D1457136

UNIVERSITY OF WINNIPEG
LIBRARY
515 Portage Avenue
Winnipeg, Manitoba R3B 2E9

DISCARDED

Three Honest Men

Published by arrangement with the
British Broadcasting Corporation

PS
78
·F74
1980

PHILIP FRENCH

THREE HONEST MEN

EDMUND WILSON

F. R. LEAVIS

LIONEL TRILLING

a critical mosaic

CARCANET NEW PRESS
MANCHESTER

First published in Great Britain in 1980
by Carcanet New Press
330 Corn Exchange Buildings
Manchester M4 3BG
© Copyright 1980 Philip French: Introductory and link material
© Copyright 1980 for recorded submissions resides with the
contributors
SBN 85635 2993
All rights reserved
The drawings by Richard Wilson are reproduced by kind permission
of the editor of the Spectator, where they were first published.

Printed in Great Britain
by Billings, Guildford and Worcester

Contents

Introduction
by Philip French

This book contains the slightly revised transcripts of three radio programmes I have compiled and presented over the past five years. Each was undertaken quite separately, the Edmund Wilson and Lionel Trilling portraits as delayed obituaries, the F. R. Leavis as an eightieth birthday tribute in 1975. This last was rebroadcast the night after his death some three years later, striking a peculiarly warm and charitable note in the often rancorous chorus that echoed through the press that week.

Intellectual portraits of this kind have been made possible through the cultural ambience created by the BBC Third Programme (and its successor, Radio Three), for which I have worked since the early 1960s, and the freedom afforded by magnetic tape. Radio Three assumes that there is an audience around Britain interested in sitting down for an hour or so to listen to a variety of people talking about men of letters. The tape recorder makes it possible to record often quite extensive interviews from which extracts of varying sizes can be carved and composed into these mosaic portraits.

The suggestion that I should undertake them myself, rather than merely produce them with a specialist literary critic or historian as compiler and presenter, came in each case from Stephen Hearst, Controller of Radio Three 1972–8, and from George Fischer, then and now the head of Radio Talks and Documentary Programmes. As I was neither an academic nor a professional literary critic, they reasoned that I would be more inclined to embark upon a course of inquiry among specialist informants with a mind that was at least partially open. I would be fuelled of course by an interest in the subjects and by an amateur acquaintance with the authors' works, lives and reputations. My enthusiasm for each project was in fact more than slight for I had long been fascinated by all three men and had been on friendly terms with Lionel Trilling since the mid-1960s.

I first came across their writings as a grammar school sixth-former in Bristol thirty years ago. F. R. Leavis's *Scrutiny* was still appearing then, but it was a well-thumbed and rebound school library edition of his *Culture and Environment* that I first read. This book profoundly shaped my rather puritanical views about the arts and society, though I took from it a stronger political message than Leavis and his co-author Denys Thompson intended. *Culture and Environment* was put into my hands either by the school's senior English teacher, the late Fred Perry (who showed me at the age of fifteen how to read, and how to take pleasure in reading), or by a recent arrival (now the Bristol Grammar School senior English master) Derek Lucas, who had come straight from Cambridge. They both commended *Axel's Castle* to me and I regret to say that until 1975, when in a fit of well-justified remorse I returned it, the school's library copy was in my possession, thus possibly depriving several generations of sixth-formers from making its acquaintance. However, it was not that book, which took me some years to appreciate, but rather the recently published collections of Wilson's literary journalism – *Classics and Commercials* and *The Shores of Light* – that attracted me to Wilson, and indeed to the idea of literary journalism.

Lionel Trilling, on the other hand, I came across almost by accident while reading the final issue (the Fortieth) of John Lehmann's *Penguin New Writing*, the first copy of that journal to come my way. In the photogravure supplement were portraits of recent American contributors to *Penguin New Writing*, among them Paul Bowles, J. F. Powers, Saul Bellow, Eudora Welty, Nelson Algren and Tennessee Williams, all soon to become favourite writers of mine. The last-named was the only one I had previously heard of. They were preceded, however, by a photograph of a handsome grey-haired man in his forties, standing with his back to a wall of books, smiling sardonically, his hands thrust into the pockets of a grey suit, wearing a black tie and smoking a cigarette. Unlike the others he was given a title – 'Professor Lionel Trilling' the caption read. He looked to me the very ideal of the intellectual, and I was not surprised to discover much later on my first visit to America that his appearance had influenced the demeanour of many of my near contemporaries on US campuses. Consequently I sought out the earlier edition of *Penguin New Writing* to which he had contributed and came across 'Of this time, of that place', and imagined its sympathetic academic hero Joseph Howe as looking like Trilling. I thus thought of him initially as a writer of fiction and was therefore disappointed to find that a novel, and another story 'The other Margaret', constituted almost all the fiction he had written. It was a long time, incidentally, before I became aware that he was a Jew, and a longer one before I understood the significance of this in his career.

My last year at school coincided with the demise of *Scrutiny* and the publication of *The Common Pursuit*, the appearance of Trilling's *The Liberal Imagination*, and the belated arrival in Britain of Wilson's *Memoirs of Hecate County*, borne in on a breeze of undeserved notoriety. I was at this point changing my direction – from the prospect of studying English and embarking on a career of teaching, to that of jurisprudence and a career in the law. Leavis, Trilling and Wilson were therefore to be my reading for pleasure, and they served to show me that criticism is an activity in no way inferior to so-called creation. On the contrary, I became convinced that criticism could indeed be superior to that which it fed on, a possibly questionable belief, but one reinforced by reading George Orwell, another abiding favourite from that time, and the theatrical criticism of Max Beerbohm. Moreover, being a rather late developer at school, and being one of the so-called 'interested intelligent laymen' whom the Third Programme was established to address, I have usually been led to writers by critics rather than the other way round. To mention random examples, it was Trilling who introduced me to Forster and to a serious consideration of Matthew Arnold, Wilson who sent me to Kipling and John O'Hara, Leavis who directed my attention to *The Secret Agent* and *Under Western Eyes* when only Conrad's sea stories were fashionable.

My interest, then, in these three men is that of someone from outside the academic world, one who was surprised when he came across Stanley Edgar Hyman's invaluable 'study in the methods of modern literary criticism', *The Armed Vision*, in its mid-1950s paperback edition, to discover that neither Trilling nor Leavis was given more than passing mention and that Wilson had been dropped from the abridged version. The book's ten chapters were given over to Yvor Winters, T. S. Eliot, Van Wyck Brooks, Constance Rourke, Maud Bodkin, Caroline Spurgeon, R. P. Blackmur, William Empson, I. A. Richards and Kenneth Burke. I came to appreciate, of course, that they did not have techniques, methods and theories to be extrapolated and taught; they could only be read for their insights and judgments. Now that even more elaborate critical apparatus is on the market – structuralism, semiology, neo-Marxism, Lacanian psycho-analysis, and other continental imports stocked in the neighbourhood literary delicatessen – they must seem even less useful to those seeking adequate armour with which to enter the literary fray. Bill Nichols, the editor of a recent fat anthology of film theory, *Movies and Methods* (1976), remarks on the need for methodologies: 'A method can help shape thoughts into more than that kind of bourgeois subjectivism where the sheer intelligence of the writer becomes the only criterion of value.' That statement is not without truth, but the antithesis implied is dubious. Ultimately men and minds must prevail over methods, and where they do not the insights and judgments will lack savour and individual authority. It is this aspect of Wilson's, Leavis's and Trilling's writings that led Michael Schmidt to suggest, and me to accept, the title *Three Honest Men*.

In their different ways, all three stood outside the academic world, yet remained scholarly in their cast of mind. Wilson did a little teaching but deliberately avoided regular or permanent academic commitments, and he became a scathing critic of the increasing pedantry of those assigned to edit standard editions of classic literary texts. Lionel Trilling took teaching very seriously and lived within the academic community. Yet he was closely in touch with intellectual journalism, wrote for the *New*

Yorker, was adviser to a book club, and never became involved in academic research even as a graduate student. F. R. Leavis again spent his life in the university and devoted much energy to considering what a university ought to be. But like Trilling, he had little taste for pure research and was constantly doing battle with the majority of his Cambridge colleagues.

They also had in common the fact that as the years passed they became increasingly depressed about the prospects for the state of literary culture and for the values by which they had lived. To that extent all three might be thought to have died in a melancholy frame of mind. Yet the very vigour of their late writing helped to refute or at least temper this pessimism, and to prevent it from being too powerfully engendered in their readers. I cannot imagine – or more correctly, I would not wish to contemplate – a civilization in which their work will cease to speak vitally to us, or the nature of their lives cease to be exemplary.

Trilling and Wilson wrote warmly but not effusively of each other's work. Trilling wrote generously of Leavis. Leavis early on was well disposed to both, but later turned sharply against them, writing most disparagingly for instance of Wilson's contribution to the rehabilitation of Dickens' serious reputation, and bitterly of Trilling's fair-minded comments on the 'Two Cultures' controversy. Wilson had little time for Leavis. In some passing remarks upon the 'Snow-Leavis' affair he said of Leavis: 'He's the kind of dogmatic person who inevitably antagonizes me. I can't understand making a life-or-death issue out of one's preference for this or that writer.' Elsewhere in the same book (*The Bit Between My Teeth*, 1965), Wilson takes Trilling to task in one of his pieces on the current use of English:

> In a period of moral impotence, so many things are thought of as intimidating that they are euphemistically referred to as 'massive'. I shall not present further examples except to register a feeling of horror at finding this adjective resorted to three times, and twice in the same paragraph, by Lionel Trilling in *Commentary*, in

the course of an otherwise admirable discussion of the
Snow-Leavis controversy: 'massive significance' of *The
Two Cultures*; 'massive intention' of *The Two Cultures*;
'quite massive blunder' of Snow in regard to the Victorian writers. Was Snow's essay really that huge and
weighty? If it was, perhaps then it might follow that
any blunder in it must also be massive. I myself, I am
sorry to say, have lately been described as massive. . . .

The reader of this book must remember that these are
texts of broadcasts and that a certain amount of nuance
and flavour is lost in print. If you know any of the voices,
I hope you will hear them rising from these pages. One
has to say that Wilson, Leavis and Trilling were themselves reluctant broadcasters and far from happy at the
microphone. Wilson had a strange piping voice and
turned down all but a single invitation from the BBC. The
one he accepted was to do a short talk on the Dead Sea
Scrolls for a North Region programme in the 1950s. It was
transmitted from Manchester. The Third Programme itself
decided not to rebroadcast it on the grounds, I believe,
that Wilson was not a genuine expert on the subject, and
the recording was not preserved in the BBC's archives.

F. R. Leavis broadcast occasionally in the 1940s, then
fell out with the BBC. For the rest of his life he spoke
bitterly about the Corporation, holding the Third Programme to be an agent and symptom of cultural decline.
He too was an indifferent broadcaster, though he was
often invited to speak. Fortunately he did allow the Third
Programme to record and broadcast his address to the
1968 Cheltenham Festival. This is now in the BBC
Archives and I was able to quote from it. I did not consult
Dr Leavis while preparing my programme, but let him
know a couple of weeks before transmission that it was
going out. I received a simple acknowledgement written
in his own hand, and heard indirectly that he had neither
been embarrassed nor gravely displeased by the
programme.

I first met Lionel Trilling when he gave his Henry Sedg-
wick Memorial Lecture at Cambridge in 1965. We recorded
it as delivered before a distinguished audience at Newn-

ham College, but he was unhappy about both his per-
formance and the lecture itself. He radically recast his text
for publication (for *Encounter* first, then in *Beyond Culture*)
and so we arranged to make a studio version at Broadcasting House one Saturday afternoon. It was the day the
American horse 'Jay Trump' won the Grand National, and
I mentioned this to him when we met (our first proper
meeting) saying that I ought to have backed it. To my
surprise I found he was not only unaware of the race
being run that day but had only the haziest idea of what
the Grand National was. Naturally therefore he was somewhat bemused to find himself in the company of a gam-
bler (if only a potential one) discussing his Cambridge
lecture in a subterranean studio in Portland Place. The
task of recording went slowly, with many stops and re-
takes. Several times he mentioned that this was the most
boring lecture he had ever listened to, and said he was
almost putting himself to sleep. Indeed he did have, when
reading, a rather flat soporific delivery that benefited a
good deal, I'm happy to say, from the professional advice
and encouragement I was able to provide. Eventually all
was done, and he was sincerely astonished to hear I
thought the result worth broadcasting. He left me free to
suggest to the BBC that the lecture be dropped altogether,
or to cut as much as, and wherever, I thought fit. In the
event his complete text was transmitted, the programme
running sixty-six minutes, the longest scripted talk I (and,
so far as I know, any of my colleagues) have ever recorded
in the studio. According to the BBC's Audience Research
Department, the lecture was heard by ·1 per cent of the
British population. Had those listeners gathered at Wem-
bley the stadium would have been at least half-full and
possibly packed out. By contrast, the recording of our
conversation about Edmund Wilson, from which the
extracts in the Wilson programme came, went very
smoothly indeed. We just slipped away from a lunchtime
gathering at the Trillings' Oxford flat where they were
living in the academic year 1972–3, taped the interview in
a quiet back room, and returned to a company that had
scarcely noticed our absence.

I should like to thank Stephen Hearst and George

Fischer for the freedom they gave me in making these programmes, Michael Schmidt for not only saying they would make a book (people are always telling me that) but actually offering to publish it, and Helen Ramsbotham for her work on editing the texts for publication. I must also express once more my thanks to those who contributed to the three portraits, and for allowing their words to be printed again. Much shortened versions of each appeared in *The Listener* (the Wilson programme on 20 September 1973, the Leavis on 24 July 1975, the Trilling on 15 December 1977) and the whole of the Trilling in *Poetry Nation Review*.

At the end I have appended some biographical notes on the contributors, pointing out where they have written on Wilson, Leavis and Trilling. The bibliographies on my three subjects are highly selective. More extensive ones can be found in *Contemporary Literary Critics* edited by Elmer Borklund (1977) and elsewhere.

Edmund Wilson, 1895–1972

PHILIP FRENCH: Edmund Wilson was many things: critic, playwright, novelist, poet, editor, reporter, social observer, historian. When he died in June 1972 at the age of seventy-seven, most of his obituarists, subsuming all these roles under one single title, referred to him as America's 'pre-eminent man-of-letters'. It is this side of his life that I want to concentrate on here.

His background was of course important. Edmund Wilson came from a family that could trace its ancestors to eighteenth-century British and Dutch immigrants. His forebears were Presbyterians and Calvinists, largely professional people. His father was a successful lawyer who served for a period as Attorney-General of New Jersey, and it was from him that Wilson inherited his love of travel, his questioning nature, his belief in social justice. His childhood – as an only child – was privileged but far from entirely happy. His parents were frequently in conflict; his father was subject to appalling periods of depression, suffered from acute hypochondria, and spent lengthy stretches in sanatoriums. His mother became deaf at an early age; and while she long outlived her husband, who died in 1923, she never took much interest in her son's writing.

Wilson's education was fairly typical for his class and background: he went to a private preparatory school and then on to Princeton, which proved an important shaping experience through the influence of his teachers and of his contemporaries, who included the poet John Peale Bishop and F. Scott Fitzgerald. His career as a writer began at Princeton, and his first writing job was as a reporter on the New York *Sun*, which he left when America entered the First World War, to serve in the ranks with a hospital unit in France. After the war he joined the magazine *Vanity Fair* as managing editor, and subsequently worked until the early 1930s as an associate editor of the liberal literary and political weekly *New Republic*. He hadn't drifted into writing; he had consciously embarked on a literary career, as he explained in his autobiographical work *A Prelude*. He knew, he wrote, that his family of lawyers and preachers and doctors 'had their doubts about me and that in order to prove myself I should have to show that a writer could become a successful professional'.

By the late 1920s Wilson was already something of a heroic figure in New York's Greenwich Village through his verse, his criticism and his editorial power. He was then working on what became his first major book: *Axel's Castle*, a study of the symbolists and European avant-garde literature. The American critic Lionel Trilling, some ten years Wilson's junior, was himself starting out as a critic at this time. To him Wilson, as he later wrote, 'seemed to propose and to realize the ideal of the literary life'. I asked Professor Trilling what kind of initial impression Wilson made upon him in 1929.

LIONEL TRILLING: Wilson wasn't intimidating then, as he later became, when everybody found him so; indeed my first memory of him is deeply at odds with later recollections. He came to look like a sort of nineteenth-century British ship captain, or like Henry James – a peremptory and commanding figure, very much in that style; but when I first went to see him at the *New Republic*, to ask him for some books to review, he was terribly shy and rather withdrawn and self-defensive, by no means as assertive and forceful as in later years. Wilson appeared to me then as very gentle and rather dim; in fact his new persona almost amounted to a transformation.

FRENCH: This new persona was the face that the public came to know, the man who would later answer letters with a printed card stating that 'Mr Wilson regrets that it is impossible for him to . . . write introductions . . . make speeches . . . give interviews . . . supply personal information about himself' and so on, with a little tick in the requisite box. Yet behind this aloof patrician exterior there was an immense personal warmth, which we will hear about later from several people who knew him – indeed this warmth is always evident in his work, I think. Sticking to the 1920s for the moment, however, and turning to the last book published in his lifetime –*Upstate*, the journals kept during the summers he spent in the old family home he restored in Talcottville in northern New York State – we find Wilson referring to himself there at the age of sixty-five as 'a man of the twenties' – the decade of hope and excitement dominated by H. L. Mencken, who greatly influenced Wilson, by his friend Scott Fitzgerald and by Ernest Hemingway, whose importance Wilson was among the first to recognize. He was of course Fitzgerald's best and sharpest critic and in some ways the keeper of his conscience; and he did two posthumous services for the novelist, both labours of love – the skilfully edited version of the uncompleted novel *The Last Tycoon*, and the edition of Fitzgerald's essays and notebooks called *The Crack-Up*. I spoke to the poet Stephen Spender about Wilson and the twenties.

STEPHEN SPENDER: In my view, looking at him in that context, Wilson would seem to belong to a period somewhat further back than the 1920s in American history. He was rather an eighteenth-century kind of American – indeed, with his very solid appearance and his rather sparse hair one could readily imagine him in a wig, as an eighteenth-century man. His family was by origin Scots, I think, and one could sense this: he resembled one of those eighteenth-century or early nineteenth-century Scottish intellectuals at the *Edinburgh Review* – something of that sort. He was very anti-English indeed; throughout his whole career there ran a kind of polemic directed against the English, arising partly from his experience during the First World War, when he became bitterly opposed to England for having brought America into the war. Wilson was an isolationist to some extent, but also a man of the early American Republic; I don't think he greatly approved of much that had happened since Jefferson. I see him as an American of the Henry James type, looking at Europe from the outside; but his attitude was very different from that of e. e. cummings, William Carlos Williams and later Americans, who simply rejected

Europe. After all, in *Axel's Castle* he wrote primarily, indeed almost entirely, about European writers, albeit in the detached American way, which means that he adopted a firmer attitude towards tradition than a European, for whom it simply forms part of the continuity of European cultural life. Edmund Wilson certainly tended to see the tradition from the outside, rather as Henry James had done and as Eliot did later on; and in this he was, I suppose, typically American.

FRENCH: Another British author who knew Wilson well is the short story writer and critic V. S. Pritchett. Following up the American aspect of Wilson, I asked Victor Pritchett about the tradition of man of letters to which Wilson belonged.

V. S. PRITCHETT: In the first place, Wilson had something which would seem to be common to all American writers at a certain stage in their lives, the reporting instinct. Secondly, he had the general American attitude to history – that it's essential to keep records, of your own particular family, your town or whatever it is. This addiction to record is extremely strong in Americans, partly because they feel the lack of a long tradition behind them and therefore consider it their duty to pile up documents in a way that seems to us to be fact-fetishism; they have a real need to state who they are, whom they are related to and whence they came, where their relations live, what trades they follow, and so on.

Wilson's other distinction, perhaps, is that he enlarged upon this characteristic by adopting a historical attitude to criticism in literature, as it were, so that the social background of a writer at his particular time was something which he always considered very carefully. I think this was due to his early interest in socialism, and particularly to his belief (described in the *Finland Station* book) in the promise of the Russian Revolution at its outset. He was deeply interested, characteristically, in the history of socialism, but as a kind of bookish history, based on random reading rather than on documents: *Finland Station* begins with a long account of Michelet's history, for example. Wilson was a very bookish man. He was not a very good prose writer, so if by a 'man of letters' you mean a man who writes elegant prose – a sort of 'belle-lettrist' – he certainly was not that. He was a man given to caustic, plain, direct statement, who often used the vernacular phrase, usually in order to give the paragraph a punch. He was a writer of paragraphs, not of sentences. That's the main thing about his writing, I think: any paragraph as a whole is very forcible and clear, while any separate sentence is liable to sound rather broken-backed, so that he should really be read a paragraph at a time.

FRENCH: I began reading Wilson's work at more than a paragraph at a time in my last years at school when his collected essays from the twenties, thirties and forties were published in this country as *The Shores of Light* and *Classics and Commercials*. These two volumes were the first books by him I'd seen, and they opened my eyes to a range of literature and a way of looking at writers in society that were entirely new. I also liked the chunky format in which the books were published, setting them aside from other books on the library shelves – they seemed stocky, sturdy, individual, like the man himself – and I went on to get everything I could find by him. The impression made upon me by Wilson in my youth is shared, I'm happy to say, by the critic and author John Wain. In his formative years, the humanistic tradition to which Wilson belonged was what Professor Wain himself thought criticism was all about.

JOHN WAIN: Wilson is still my idea of a literary critic. If one looks around nowadays so many critics have a special technique of approaching a literary text, usually based in some way on linguistics, such as the structuralism that is popular in France. In the event, however, the effort of grasping this technique is so great that it doesn't leave its followers any time actually to read literature; they read very little, for they are so busy fitting everything into this special framework. Now Wilson, on the contrary, read incessantly, rambling here and there, for he was never afraid to appear a bit of an amateur. He was essentially the product of an era of national cultures. The way he saw it was that people invent languages, languages being

therefore creative acts shared among a whole people.
Everybody collaborates in inventing the language, and in
keeping it in order thereafter. The individual writer then
uses the language to make his statement, but it's always
to some extent a collaboration between the writer and the
society that produced him. Wilson gives you the impression that whenever he reads he is in fact travelling in
space and in time; whether in Russia, in Ancient Rome,
in England or in America, he's moving about among the
people of that nation and in those places. There isn't really
a hard and fast line between his travel writing and his
journalism, between his reporting of social scenes and his
literary criticism. It all comes down to the same thing. For
instance, in his essay on Pushkin he says: 'Reading Pushkin for the first time for a foreigner who has already read
later Russian writers, is like coming for the first time to
Voltaire after an acquaintance with later French literature.
He feels that he is testing the pure essence of something
which he has found before only in combination with other
elements.' Now this pure essence is not just the pure
essence of the personality of the writer concerned; it is
very much a matter of a certain Russian-ness, a certain
French-ness – of their time, certainly, but also of their
country, of their place.

This element was a great strength in Wilson's criticism,
because it meant that he was free to enjoy what he
enjoyed without trying to match it up with his opinions.
Take *Axel's Castle*, for instance: this is of course a book
about the great European symbolist poets and novelists,
and it is a very brilliant introduction to their work. When
he has finished it, Wilson – who at that moment was very
left-wing, deeply committed to radical socialist solutions
for what was then seen as the collapse of American cap-
italism – Wilson turns round and says in the Epilogue that
it won't do, that symbolism won't work and shouldn't be
introduced into America, that it's not right for America;
it is not right for the future and it is not the direction that
the literary mind should take. And he's perfectly entitled
to that opinion. Yet throughout the body of the book he
has discussed the work of these great symbolist poets and
novelists with such interest, such responsiveness, such

loving attention, indicating that symbolism most certainly *will* do! This change of front is just like the reaction of people travelling. The European mind produced symbolism, symbolism produced masterpieces of literature; we enjoy them, we travel there and come back again. It's perfectly open to Wilson when he gets back to say: 'Nevertheless I wouldn't like to see American writers go the same way'. This enables the traveller always to be generous and appreciative without feeling that he has got to sell out his own particular values.

FRENCH: That is John Wain's view. There is some problem, however, about Wilson's particular stance. He never consistently sustained a Marxist position – not even in his brilliant series of reports on America in the 1930s Depression, first published as *The American Jitters* and later revised and expanded as *The American Earthquake*. He launched provocative ideas and theories throughout his life, yet in no programmatic fashion. His collection of essays *The Wound and the Bow*, for instance, is informed by a thesis – inspired by Sophocles' *Philoctetes* – that the artist is a psychically injured person and that society must accept this wound as the price of his art. That book incidentally, published in 1941, was years ahead of fashionable opinion in its revaluation of both Charles Dickens and Rudyard Kipling. But what part did ideas play in Wilson's work? The American writer and publisher, Jason Epstein, a close friend of Wilson in his later years, has a pretty clear view of this subject.

JASON EPSTEIN: Wilson was impatient with metaphysics, with anything that wasn't concrete, that couldn't be discovered and proved, that you couldn't touch or see or pick up in your hands and look at. He never thought of himself as an intellectual; that's a description he would never have used, indeed he made fun of the word and scoffed at it. He saw himself as an explainer, as a journalist, in fact; as someone who would confront a difficult, obscure subject – say the Dead Sea Scrolls, or political ideas during the Civil War as they were expressed in fiction at the time – and who would tackle this as a puzzle to be solved, just as a sculptor sets himself the problem

of finding out what is within a block of stone. He would
then chip away at it determinedly, reading everything
relevant, questioning everybody concerned, travelling
around, learning the necessary languages if he had to –
Hebrew and Hungarian at one point: he even learnt or
began to learn the language of the Iroquois because he
was interested in their situation (the Iroquois Indians in
upper New York State). He had no patience with abstract
ideas as such, nor with people who did have such
interests.

In a sense Wilson was much more a man of the Old
Testament than of the New. He had a completely untheo-
retical mind, terribly intolerant of writers like Thomas
Mann, whom I once tried to discuss with him: he just
brushed Mann aside, and he couldn't bear Kafka, for the
same reason. He didn't know why the characters in Kafka
were so troubled: why couldn't they just solve their problems, like anybody else? What's bothering them? He
thought they were weak, letting themselves get all mixed
up with silly things. It is perfectly obvious, according to
Wilson, what K in *The Trial* should have done: he should
have gone to a good lawyer and got himself out of that
mess. That is the way he dealt with ideas; he certainly
understood them and could cope with them. There was
nothing he couldn't explain, propounding the most
abstruse Hegelian notions in the simplest language, as in
To the Finland Station.

Metaphysics presented no problem for Wilson, therefore; he understood 'all that stuff'; but such ideas were
always artefacts for him, never things that he himself
subscribed to or was willing to debate with other people.
He saw them as historical objects rather than things you
believe in or debate for their own sake.

FRENCH: This attitude that Jason Epstein speaks of led to
Wilson occupying a rather solitary, individual position;
and while later on I want to go further into the nature of
his enduring reputation, I'd like to include at this point a
personal comment on his influence from Lionel Trilling.

TRILLING: Wilson's career is full of contradictions. He
was always respected, certainly, but it is interesting that

most of the academic critics, though respecting him, never
seemed to discover in him anything of special importance.
No group ever turned to him, and I believe this was
exactly how he wanted it to be, for Wilson never formed
a school. I don't think he influenced anyone except
through his example. I know his ideas never had any
influence on me, for instance. I listened to what he had
to say and perhaps would borrow from him, but he never
shaped my thought after my very first years. Most people
would say the same, I think, though with all respect for
what he did, which was to bring an enormous lucidity
and intelligence and commonsense to the study of literature. Wilson was never fully speculative, but he always
brought a very precise critical intelligence to bear upon
the work of the creative mind.

The way in which Wilson did influence me, I suppose,
was that he, more than anyone else, taught me the virtues
of simplicity of writing, which I don't always achieve but
try to attain. Also he gave me the desire to communicate
not only with professionals but with intelligent people
generally.

FRENCH: Lionel Trilling's point about communicating
with intelligent people generally is crucial to an understanding of Wilson – and to understanding why perhaps
he means so much to so many people not engaged in the
professional study of literature, or history, or other academic disciplines. Wilson came in the 1940s to acquire a
platform as critic and reporter for one of the glossiest,
most affluent, yet least easily categorized American magazines, *The New Yorker*. It was there that Wilson launched
his controversial series of essays on the detective story –
including one with a title that has almost entered the
language: 'Who Cares Who Killed Roger Ackroyd?'. He
continued to contribute to other journals – his notes on
the degradation of the English language were once a regular feature of the *New Statesman*, and in the final years of
his life much of his most important writing appeared in
the *New York Review of Books*. But the critic and essayist
George Steiner attaches great significance to this particular
platform.

GEORGE STEINER: For more than a quarter of a century Edmund Wilson was very closely associated with the *New Yorker*, and there are a couple of points worth making in this connection. The length of his articles (which were often written with a future book in view) was one of the *New Yorker* features. He was allowed ten thousand words for a book review, which would then become an essay on the subject as a whole and in which he would often go much beyond the book in hand to start a theme. For instance, *The Dead Sea Scrolls* and all the essays on American Civil War literature in *Patriotic Gore* (which is, I think, his masterpiece) were originally *New Yorker* pieces. No other magazine that I know of would have allowed and encouraged their peculiar format, which we last find in the nineteenth-century English journals – the enormous reviews of Macaulay and his contemporaries. To take a negative view, it might be said that some of Edmund Wilson's self-indulgent length, cantankerous detail, quirky pursuit of detours from the main argument, was also made possible by this format.

In his early journalism Wilson wrote much more briefly – what we would see as very short book reviews. With the *New Yorker* he could take up to a year at a time and do these enormous, very learned essays. There is a further point I should like to make: the *New Yorker* has an obsession with the minute fact, it is famous for this (its adversaries find this pedantic, while those who like it look for this very trait). Whether it is dealing with American baseball or the amount of oil that flows in a motor, the *New Yorker* prides itself on a curious mammoth nineteenth-century encyclopaedic obsession with exact detail. And much in Edmund Wilson's ripe manner reflects this haughty pedantry – that is the only way I can put it, very arrogant pedantry. This is also psychologically important. His relations with the university world were always ambivalent, for he knew he was not fully accepted there for the great scholar that he was; Wilson in turn considered most academics less good at the job than himself – less good at research, less definitive and massive in their work. I would emphasize, therefore, that the *New Yorker* and its editors defined for him this extremely special middle position.

FRENCH: George Steiner has in some ways inherited Wilson's critical mantle in the literary section of *The New Yorker*. As he pointed out, Wilson's 1955 book *The Scrolls from the Dead Sea* was made possible by *The New Yorker*, which enabled him to visit Israel in the early 1950s and then return twelve years later for another series of articles to bring his first book up to date, an arduous journey for a man in his seventies.

Several major books came between these two – on the American Indians, the American Civil War, on Canada and Canadian literature – and one is astonished by the way in which Wilson kept up throughout the whole period with the complicated scholarship on the subject. His first book on the Scrolls was the most commercially successful and popular he ever wrote, and also the most controversial. The archaeologist Yigael Yadin of the Hebrew University in Jerusalem is among the foremost experts in this field. I asked Professor Yadin how he saw this aspect of Wilson's work.

YIGAEL YADIN: It is something of an irony that the Dead Sea Scrolls themselves were not found by archaeologists. In fact they were discovered by the Bedouin, and their importance was brought to the knowledge of the world at large, again not by an archaeologist but by a scholarly amateur, so to speak – Edmund Wilson. Were it not for the Bedouin on the one hand and Wilson on the other, I'm not so sure that the subject of the Dead Sea Scrolls would have been known at all. I think Wilson's contribution to the world-wide interest and popular understanding of the Dead Sea Scrolls was immense at the time, because he sensed very early in the research proceedings that perhaps one of the most important aspects is the relation between the writings of the Essenes – The Dead Sea Scrolls people, that is to say – and the birth and beginning of Christianity. Wilson sensed this at a time when the whole matter was just becoming apparent. Discussion amongst scholars was taking place here and there,

but many of these scholars were shy of jumping to conclusions or of making their conclusions better known.

I wouldn't like to put Wilson in any particular religious
denomination but I think that his main interest in the
Scrolls at the beginning, what intrigued and appealed to
him most, was exactly how Christianity was born out of
Judaism, what were the factors influencing this question.
If you re-read his first book on the Scrolls, even the second
one, in fact, you can sense quite clearly that he tends to
return to that particular problem. It would be true to say
that Wilson contributed not only to the fact that the Dead
Sea Scrolls became better known in the lay world but also,
though not himself a scholar from the technical point of
view, that he influenced some scholars in the way they
dealt with the Scrolls, because he was very provocative in
his writings. He was trying to define the views of some
scholars more boldly than they themselves dared, perhaps, and this created fresh controversy. I would say,
therefore, that Wilson's contribution was of real importance to the actual scholarly work on the Dead Sea Scrolls.
Wilson's personality was indeed a strange, rare combination: I would describe him as an amateur in the nine-
teenth- or eighteenth-century meaning of the word, at
that period when amateurs really knew far more than
strictly professional people.

FRENCH: During the years after World War II, Wilson
turned away from current literature for the most part, to
concentrate upon that of the past, and to devote himself,
as we have seen, to major historical enterprises. This was
widely resented by the younger writers of the day, and
tended for a while to establish something of a gulf
between Wilson and themselves, between their generation and his, for he had come in the literary forum to be
the informal tribune of Fitzgerald, Hemingway, Dos Pas-
sos and the other figures of the so-called 'lost generation'.
One of these new writers spoke out about it in a forceful
essay called 'Ladder to Heaven: novelists and critics of
the forties', signing with the pseudonym 'Libra'. The
author was later revealed as the novelist Gore Vidal, who
recalled for me how he felt at the time.

GORE VIDAL: When we came upon the scene – the so-called War Novelists of the 1940s – Edmund Wilson was certainly the major critical figure in the country, I would say. We knew him first, I suppose, as the friend of Scott Fitzgerald; *The Crack-Up* was a very valuable book for a whole generation. I remember that we were all quite interested in what his reaction would be to us, the coming generation of writers, as we proudly saw ourselves – what Wilson would say about us, how he would relate us to the writers of the twenties and thirties, whom he knew best. In fact, to our amazement, he did not take the slightest interest in any of us! He wrote one review of Carson McCullers, I think it was of *Reflections in a Golden Eye*; it was a rather poor review and not a very intelligent one. He tended to like Charles Jackson, an estimable writer but not someone we considered central to our great generation; he did a very fine piece on John Horne Burns, on *The Gallery*, and with that I think I have practically named every post-war American writer that Wilson dealt with. I remember a gradual sense of shock and disillusionment, and a degree of irritability: here was, if not the best, certainly the most powerful literary critic in the United States, writing regularly in *The New Yorker*, and all he was doing was to write about Edna St Vincent Millay, Scott Fitzgerald and Ernest Hemingway! He caused us a good deal of distress at that time. Later, as we began to get his range – his new range – then of course we saw the valuable work he was doing, particularly in writing about the American past, about the Civil War, in that book of his called *Patriotic Gore* (unfortunately titled for me – if ever again I'm referred to as Un-patriotic Gore, I will probably write a letter to the editor, if not to my solicitor . . .). This insight revealed a whole new aspect of Wilson, as a general critic of the culture, which we had not realized in 1946, '47, '48, or into the early fifties.

FRENCH: During the period of which Gore Vidal speaks a major crisis was quietly building up in Edmund Wilson's life. He was totally oblivious to the time-bomb that was ticking away beneath him, which exploded with devastating effect in the late fifties, involving him in consider-

able embarrassment, humiliation and continual harassment at the hands of the United States Internal Revenue Service. It brought together his personal life and his public stance in a quite extraordinary fashion.

EPSTEIN: As Wilson wrote in his book *The Cold War and the Income Tax*, he didn't pay his income tax for a period of years – perhaps in neglect, perhaps wilfully, perhaps on principle – most likely a combination of all three. This period dated from the mid-forties, probably through the early fifties, when incidentally he had practically no income. . . . When I first met him (in 1952, I guess it was), Wilson had no money at all to speak of, which astonished me: here was someone esteemed as our leading man of letters by everybody who counted, and he was penniless! Nor did this seem to bother him; he never complained, but managed to live a good sort of patrician upper-class life without money up in Cape Cod. I suppose it didn't occur to him that he *couldn't* have paid his income tax, for during those years he had no money.

Wilson's attitude to his predicament goes back of course to his old Copperhead, anti-union, anti-federalist position. Why should he pay money to a government that he considered illegitimate, that had been imposed on the American people without their specific consent? So, partly out of inadvertence, of poverty, of anger, partly on principle, he didn't pay it. Inevitably, he was affected by the consequences: he got caught, and this was very painful. He became involved in all kinds of messy paper-work; I remember the house was full of cancelled cheques in those days, with lawyers and accountants coming and going. . . . It was his good wife Elena who pulled the whole thing together for him, and somehow he managed to extricate himself. But I think Wilson was probably right, in the little book he wrote about his income tax problems, to say that fundamentally his reason for not having paid his taxes was one of principle, because he felt the government of the day really had no right to make such demands on its citizens for such hideous ends. He didn't like the idea of the Cold War, he didn't like the way the money was being spent or the way the government interfered in every-

body's life. He was full of contradictions, like everybody else in America.

Wilson undoubtedly supported most of what we think of as New Deal programmes, though he didn't like Roosevelt, by the way; I'm sure he was in favour of government support for poor people, and so on, yet at the same time he resented, as some conservative Republicans claim to resent, the intrusion of government into people's private lives. He was a very stubborn, difficult old man about these things, and as I say very much a Copperhead from beginning to end.

FRENCH: Those were Jason Epstein's views. I should perhaps explain that the term 'Copperhead' was the epithet applied during the Civil War to Northerners who sympathized with the Southern cause and the right to secede from the Union – an attitude underlying Wilson's *Patriotic Gore*. While Wilson was correcting the proofs of his diatribe *The Cold War and the Income Tax* in 1963, he was approached by Arthur Schlesinger Jr to see whether he would accept one of President John F. Kennedy's newly instituted Freedom Medals. He warned the administration about his impending book and later learned that Kennedy had brushed aside a sixteen-page memorandum from the Internal Revenue Department objecting to the proposed award. 'This is not an award for good conduct but for literary merit', said the President.

Reverting to Wilson in less difficult mood, I spoke to John Wain about the occasion in the mid-fifties when he visited Wilson to write an article for the *Observer*.

WAIN: Wilson was a man always ready to set out on a journey to another country of the mind. When I first met him, I went to stay with him in the old house in Upstate New York that he was so proud of, in a rather Yeatsian way, talking about his family, his ancestors and so on; I took a parcel of books that I thought might interest him, as a present. We sat up until a normal time, then I went to bed. In the morning he got up very late and was rather hung-over, and it turned out that after I'd gone to bed he had torn the parcel open and had devoured those books: he was the sort of man who gobbled up books. At that

time he was well over sixty, but he was still excited by a
new book, a fresh literary experience. He had sat up late
reading with a bottle beside him and had finished up with
a hang-over, so he was very sorry for himself. But I
thought it was very beautiful. I felt that here was the
Edmund Wilson I had gone to see, and that unlike so
many literary men he was not a disappointment. I had
been slightly apprehensive, expecting difficulties, because
he was well known as an Anglophobe, certainly politically: in the late thirties, for instance, he used to go about
breathing fire and saying things like 'There's going to be
a war and England is going to be defeated, and a good
job too'. But in actual fact there was nobody Wilson got
on better with than an English man of letters, because
there was no barrier – none of that subtle readjustment
one so often has to make with the present generation of
Americans who see things from a point of view in which
England doesn't much matter one way or the other.
Whereas in Wilson's case, even when he was being
vicious about England it was because he was so closely
tied to that Eastern Seaboard tradition which is itself an
offshoot of the tradition of this country.

FRENCH: One way and another Wilson had good reason
to be confirmed in his Anglophobia, which reached its
shrillest pitch in his account of his immediately post-war
travels on this side of the Atlantic, *Europe Without Baedeker*,
a book that occasioned a ludicrous onslaught on him by
the British popular press. His remarks there upon English
manners still strike me as shrewd and just. It was during
the visit that John Wain has just described that he himself
played a curious role in triggering off a series of *New
Yorker* articles by Wilson that was eventually published in
1959 as the book *Apologies to the Iroquois*, a thinnish work
in some ways when re-read today but characteristically
years ahead of fashionable concern.

WAIN: I take a harmless pleasure – I hope it's a harmless
pleasure – in the fact that I am mentioned a few times in
Wilson's work. The occasion I am most proud of is when
I don't appear as me but just as 'a person from Porlock'.
I'm a "young English writer' who came to stay with Wil-

son, and while Wilson and this 'young English writer'
(viz. and to wit myself) were driving about the country-
side the YEW said to him 'What about the Indians? Are
there many of them left? and what sort of way of life do
they have?' To which Wilson replied that he didn't think
there were many left, and as far as he knew they had no
particular way of life. Then after I'd gone he sat down
and thought about it; he worked up the subject and got
interested, and that was the reason why he wrote that
book. It is quite impossible to say whether if I hadn't gone
to see him he would ever have started on it, but I daresay
this might have happened – the next person would have
asked him the questions, if I hadn't. It was still possible
to start his mind working in an unforeseen direction, even
when he was well over sixty; and I think all these things,
showing his enterprise and resilience, are a great credit to
him.

FRENCH: Such books as *Apologies to the Iroquois*, his dis-
illusioned contribution to the centenary celebrations of the
Civil War *Patriotic Gore*, his essay 'Reflections at Sixty', all
suggest a very real melancholy on Wilson's part about the
state of the nation. When *The Cold War and the Income Tax*
appeared there was a tendency to dismiss the book as
another choleric outburst by an angry, disgruntled old
man who has failed to come to terms with modern bureau-
cratic society and to fulfil his obligations to it. Gore Vidal,
however, reacted very differently – he had been among
the first writers of a liberal persuasion to recover from the
Kennedy euphoria of the early sixties. Reviewing *The Cold
War and the Income Tax* in 1963 Vidal observed: 'Mr Wilson's pamphlet might be just the jolt we need. Not since
Tom Paine has the drum of polemic sounded with such
urgency through the land, and it is to be hoped that every
citizen of the United States will read this book'.

Vidal and Wilson have a good deal in common both in
their social backgrounds and also in the themes that they
pursued during the past twenty years, including their
despair over what they saw as a burgeoning American
imperialism. I asked Gore Vidal how he felt about this
parallel and about Wilson's attitude to America.

VIDAL: I certainly had enormous sympathy with Wilson as a writer throughout his career, and with his growing melancholy about the American scene; and I certainly wish he had lived long enough to see the Watergate spectacle, because he would have had a great deal to say about that. Wilson and I were both rooted in the Puritan tradition, and had that sense of America being something very special which was shared by everybody until, let us say, twenty-five years ago, perhaps. To my mind, the despair you note in Wilson's writing is not singular; he thought that the great experiment was going bad, that we now have forms which have outlasted their use, that we have a whole national philosophy which is just a cover-up for ordinary greed of a sort that is positively European. In other words, we have lived long enough to see the great experiment look pretty sad. Naturally one's views are coloured by one's age – my melancholy in middle-age is not as dark as Wilson's melancholy in old age – but what kept him going, I believe, and keeps me at work too, is a sense of the contradiction in things, of the sheer excitement that stupidity can cause in a professional watcher of his fellow-countrymen; and behind Wilson's direct commentaries there was always this extraordinary mind, capable of adopting simultaneously so many different attitudes. It was Wilson, I think, who quoted Scott Fitzgerald, saying how difficult it was to live with a contradiction, that Americans could never tolerate a sense of yes and no, it always had to be yes *or* no; thus we have our nay-sayers on the one hand and our yea-sayers on the other. Wilson himself, however, *did* have this sense of the balance between yes and no – perhaps the highest wisdom that a critic can achieve, and he certainly achieved it.

FRENCH: One can easily gain from Wilson's writings the impression of a very difficult and disenchanted man, and indeed we know that he cannot have been an easy person to get along with. He was married four times – the most turbulent of his marriages being his years with his third wife, Mary McCarthy, the events of which are generally considered to have been the inspiration for her novel *A*

Charmed Life (1955) – though it was Edmund Wilson who encouraged her to turn to fiction in the first place: he was the guiding force behind her impressive début as a creative writer, *The Company She Keeps* (1942). His last, and happy, marriage to Elena Thornton, continued from 1946 until his death.

Yet was Wilson as detached and disenchanted as he made out in, say, 'Reflections at Sixty'? Not according to Jason Epstein.

EPSTEIN: He maintained the pretence of detachment and disenchantment, even to himself, but I doubt that it was true – in fact I know it wasn't true. Everything interested him; he had a voracious curiosity about all that happened in the world, such as I have never seen in anyone else. He kept up with everyday political matters and all the new books, of course – he claimed not to read new fiction at all, but in fact he did. He didn't pay much attention to it for the most part, yet he certainly knew what was going on.

Wilson retired from the everyday world, to some extent, when he went to live in Wellfleet up in Cape Cod – a remote community, especially in winter when nobody goes there. In the summer time, when the tourists descend on Cape Cod, he would go to Talcottville, an even more isolated place in Upper New York State – unspeakably remote. This was not in order to detach himself from the world, however, but to guarantee his privacy, for he worked very hard and needed a lot of peace and quiet. Wilson was the kind of man who attracted visitors, many of them uninvited. He was very gregarious, and he probably felt that his gregariousness would undo him as a writer; therefore he put himself out of people's reach, locked up and isolated, so that he could finish his articles and books.

Edmund Wilson was not any more detached or disenchanted than, say, E. M. Forster, who also pretended to be out of the world; Wilson wasn't really cut off for a moment, he knew all about what was going on. He was even interested in everyday politics; for instance he was wearing a McGovern button at one point just before he

died – he didn't approve of the Republicans at all. It's not
in the least true that Wilson was detached and disenchanted, difficult or rude, or any of the things that people
say about him – he was nothing of the sort, but on the
contrary extremely friendly and open, curious about
everything and a great cross-examiner when one visited
him in Wellfleet or Talcottville. For instance, he would sit
me down and ask a list of questions about everyday things
– New York literary gossip, who's writing what, who's
seeing whom, who was up, who was down – he just
couldn't get enough of this. The questions were largely
disingenuous, of course, because he knew all the answers,
and would hardly let me finish my reply before complet-
ing it for me himself and going on to his next question,
which he would also answer. He certainly knew what was
up.

FRENCH: Jason Epstein's impression of Wilson in his last
years is very much confirmed by V. S. Pritchett, who told
me about his unforgettable final meeting with Wilson in
the autumn of 1971, not long before his death and after
he had experienced a period of very bad health.

PRITCHETT: The last time I saw Edmund Wilson he was
coming down from Talcottville. The journey was very
dangerous for him, and he had to be brought down like
a baby in a car, stopping half-way, where I went and had
lunch with him. He was staying with friends and they
asked me over. Wilson was a very exacting invalid: he
wasn't allowed to have salt, so he insisted on everyone
else's food having no salt in it – things like that. He was
something of a tartar in this respect. And he was not
allowed to have food with us; we had to go up to see him.
I was very apprehensive, thinking I would see a disastrous
figure. Far from it: there he was lying on a couch with a
tartan rug over him, and the moment we came into the
room a bubble of conversation started, just like a fountain,
as gay as anything! In two minutes he was laughing – not
out loud; he never laughed very loudly, but seemed to
laugh all over his body quietly. His chest began to shake,
his stomach began to shake, his legs began to shake,
laughter seemed to be absolutely pouring down him. He

went from subject to subject, delighted by anything which was at all amusing. He appeared to me absolutely full of life. I was afraid of staying too long, knowing that one must take care not to wear out an invalid, and made an attempt to get away, but he absolutely prevented me from doing so – not only that, when at last we insisted on going, he commanded his wife, with a real imperial manner, to bring some more friends up to see him! There was in fact a great deal of gaiety about Wilson in his last years, and he thoroughly enjoyed all the rows that took place. I remember meeting him once quite suddenly in Cambridge, Massachusetts, when he said: 'I'm on the way to Harvard because I'm going to have a series of quarrels with some very recalcitrant nonconformist ministers there'. He was looking forward to the fight with tremendous eagerness.

Wilson was a combative man, you know. I wrote about one or two of his books, and each time I got a postcard or letter back from him saying: 'You made a mistake in line three; there weren't five windows broken in my house, there were only three', or something on those lines – always picking out some small point. And apparently, he did the same to other writers. He was always spotting some remark which he thought was an error. The first thing he did when you came into the room was to point out where you'd been wrong, even in your own work.

FRENCH: So far in this programme Edmund Wilson has been viewed very much as an American or as a figure in the Anglo-American culture. George Steiner, however, proposed a different approach, in which his work could be seen as all of a piece.

STEINER: If you look at the sources of Wilson's work on literature and politics, on biography and poetry, and if you look at some of his fiction in particular (which I shall turn to in a moment), you find much that relates him to the French *philosophes* and the French Enlightenment. He is a figure very like the Encyclopaedists – like Diderot, for example – writing dialogues, fables, political pamphlets, serious discourse, masses of criticism; fitting in with a French tradition of the man of letters with strong political implications, as it seems to me. Throughout French history, from Diderot on – take Sainte-Beuve, or Taine who was one of Wilson's real masters (as he says in *To the Finland Station*) – we find that the French are able to fit half-way into the university, half-way into journalism, becoming seminal and powerful presences, in a manner which the Anglo-Saxon academic and journalistic world has never really found easy.

Turning to Wilson's fiction, I like both *I Thought of Daisy* and *Memoirs of Hecate County* – particularly the latter. I think his fictional writings should be regarded in some ways as *contes philosophiques* – those philosophic satiric fables which French publicists and philosophers have always written on the side, not with any pretension to being great novelists but simply using the fictional form as an extension of the ironic argument. This is where Wilson belongs as a writer of fiction, and it's not easy to think of a similar English figure: Hazlitt didn't write a novel or stories in that fashion, whereas many French authors in the Edmund Wilson tradition, as it were, do. Wilson felt very much at home, in my view, with the arrogance, asperity, and polemic toughness of the French debating tradition of the *cause publique*. In his last years he used to say that what bored him so much about England was the lack of any passion over ideas.

I would not say much for Wilson's poetry, but I think it is extremely unjust to neglect *Hecate County*, for example, at a time when we're rediscovering Nathanael West, when we're beginning to try and find out who were the pioneers of the modern breakthrough on sexual and satiric subjects. Wilson was certainly among the early ones, for he was a man of extraordinary courage, as *Hecate County* shows – it may still be banned in New York State, though I'm not sure of this fact. He was one of the forerunners of what is now called the new freedom of open discussion. Here again he greatly resembles men like Diderot.

FRENCH: I think it would be fair to say that Wilson's creative work is not too highly regarded, and that he was disappointed by the public response to it. I'm sure that Malcolm Cowley was drawing on personal knowledge

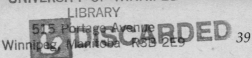
UNIVERSITY OF WINNIPEG
LIBRARY
515 Portage Avenue
Winnipeg, Manitoba R3B 2E9
DISCARDED

when he wrote, twenty years ago in his book *The Literary Situation*, that 'Edmund Wilson is a critic by popular request and almost in spite of himself, that is, in spite of the expeditions into poetry, fiction, and drama, which have never been so widely admired as his criticism.'

After George Steiner's guarded enthusiasm, John Wain's following remarks tend to reflect a more general, yet still generous attitude.

WAIN: When I read Wilson's fiction, I feel that it is a testimony to his interest in people, a kind of civilized inquisitiveness about what makes them tick, why they act as they do. Reading one of the stories in *Memoirs of Hecate County*, for instance, is not much different from reading his reminiscences of authors like Scott Fitzgerald, or for that matter his travel books, or again his criticism, which is a kind of travel book within the realm of the imagination. Indeed I have always felt that Wilson's writing was pretty much the same, whatever he was doing. In a way this could amount to a reflection upon his imaginative work, because if the latter were absolutely of the first class it would seem quite distinct from the criticism. Therefore I suppose I wind up by saying that my own view is not far from the conventional estimate of Wilson, as a major critic who had the amiable weakness of writing plays and poems and stories, except that I consider all his work to be on a level: certainly anyone who finds Wilson's criticism worth reading would be wrong to ignore the rest of his writing. Of the plays I really can't speak conclusively – I think he did lack the dramatic imagination, they don't seem to me all that good – but one should not be put off reading the poems and the fiction just by being told they are not very good; because in fact it is the same man writing, it is the same mind and it is always an interesting mind.

FRENCH: Much of Wilson's verse is very amusing and fiendishly clever in its elaborate prosody – with backward rhymes and so forth. The ingenuity makes one think of his lifelong delight in magic, and by all accounts he was a skilled conjuror with a considerable repertoire of tricks. However, one of the most frequently cited weaknesses in

his critical armoury was his alleged inability fully to
respond to poetry. A lot of his verse is of an occasional,
celebratory kind, written to entertain his family and
friends. Stephen Spender recalled one such occasion.

SPENDER: Edmund Wilson had a remarkable literary conscience. When Auden had his sixty-fifth birthday, Wilson
suddenly got hold of me and proposed that we write a
sonnet together, dedicated to and congratulating Auden,
and this was decided. I was living about five hundred
miles away from Edmund so we had to do it all by tele-
phone, or by telegram: for instance, he would send me a
telegram with one line, then two days later I would tele-
graph the following line, then within about ten minutes
I got another telegram back from Edmund with the next
line he had thought up, and so on. He was tremendously
industrious; and he had a sense of grand style, as well as
this acute literary conscience, which made him feel that
a person like Auden ought to be honoured and therefore
we should write a poem to him.

FRENCH: Most of Wilson's major writing still remains in
print – over twenty volumes of it – and since his death
there has been his revised version of *To the Finland Station*
with an alert new introduction, and a selection of his
bridge-building essays on Russian literature, *A Window on
Russia*. Moreover there should be at least another couple
of sizeable books of hitherto uncollected essays still to
come. [These have now been published and are listed in
the Bibliography.] I asked Lionel Trilling what he considered the single most important work, and what was
most likely to survive.

TRILLING: To my mind, the largest bulking and most
monumental of Wilson's works was probably his study of
the writing of history, *To the Finland Station*. I've been re-
reading that lately and I find it enormously impressive. It
is coherent and has a strong sense of the drama of developing revolutionary ideas. As to the rest, I should think
there would be perhaps three, four, five volumes of occasional pieces, fully developed essays, which are bound to
become a permanent part of the literature of America; to

me these are enormously impressive too, if not at one moment then at another. I believe that Wilson is going to exist for us, not in the same way as Matthew Arnold perhaps but rather like Sainte-Beuve – as a disinterested, detached commentator on literature in all its aspects.

FRENCH: In an eloquent memoir of Edmund Wilson written shortly after his death, Jason Epstein suggested rather lugubriously that while Wilson was spoken of as 'the dean of American letters' he was not much read, had no disciples or even imitators. I asked Mr Epstein if he still stood by this extreme opinion.

EPSTEIN: I think it was probably an over-statement for me to say that Edmund Wilson has no disciples or even imitators. Certainly Alfred Kazin, one of our leading American critics, considers himself a disciple and *is* a disciple; he is more than an imitator of Wilson obviously, but Wilson influenced him deeply, and perhaps a few other critics too. He was never widely read in America, indeed he still isn't, not because he is difficult to read – he is the simplest of writers, with perfectly translucent prose – but because he never fitted into any of the academic categories. Wilson was never a professor, for example, so he wasn't an 'eighteenth-century man' who would then be read by the other 'eighteenth-century men'; he wasn't a 'Victorian man'; and he wasn't a certified Hebrew scholar, so that when he first wrote about the Dead Sea Scrolls such scholars didn't pay much attention to him, though they came to do so later. Wilson wasn't a Marxist, he wasn't an anti-Marxist, he wasn't a this and he wasn't a that – he was very hard to pin down. I was constantly disappointed when I published his books in paperback editions – his books of essays, such as *Classics and Commercials, The Shores of Light* – to find that they were never used at all in schools, and very seldom read. We had a hard time selling them, which amazed me because I felt that a lively teacher trying to introduce his students to good prose, to show them how to write and how to think about literary and historical subjects, would want to use these books, but they didn't – simply because the books belonged to no visible category.

To my mind, Edmund Wilson's reputation will last as long as people think seriously about literature and history in this country, though it may never be widely acknowledged – probably remaining very private, in fact, like that of Henry Adams: a good reputation, but not a broad one, and that's no problem.

FRENCH: Jason Epstein's view is, I think, at least I *hope*, a little on the pessimistic side. My own view – admittedly in the face of a good deal of McLuhanesque evidence to the contrary – is that we will hear a lot more about Wilson. I also believe that he will continue to be read, and read more widely than Mr Epstein feels he now is. I'd like to end with a comment from George Steiner on what he regards as our debt to Edmund Wilson.

STEINER: As I see it, our debt to Wilson is very great on one capital point. In his books *To the Finland Station*, *Patriotic Gore*; in the essays of his last years on the Iroquois, on Vietnam, on his long battle with the American tax authorities; at his best and at his worst, he brought to the study of literature an enormous political intelligence, joining these two areas in constant interaction. This may sound like a cliché today, because who doesn't; nevertheless I believe we owe to him the example of how it should be done – with an alert awareness of the way in which literature fits into society.

There's a point I should like to emphasize here. In Wilson's last years he was contemptuous of the new jargon, emerging from the French Marxist sociology of literature in particular. He had no tolerance for it whatever, since he had been doing 'sociology of literature' in a much deeper sense, without being pompous about it, throughout his whole life. Wilson seemed to know by an extraordinary instinct how books live in men's sense of political conduct and action, how ideas are translated into action. That's what his study of Marxism and Leninism in *To the Finland Station* is about; and this is apparent even more subtly when he, beyond any other cultural historian, says: 'What did the ideas of Harriet Beecher Stowe or the other anti-slavery thinkers and novelists turn into – how did these ideas translate into the actual catastrophe of the

American Civil War?' 'Where does an idea become political action?' I believe we owe Wilson a great deal in this respect; and that in other respects too we should realize our debt to him. At his death, for instance, he was engaged in a massive study of Hungarian, a terribly difficult language. He wanted to do a book on the Hungarian poet Petöfi, having convinced himself that Petöfi was of the stature of Pushkin and should be introduced to the Western reader; and with superb intellectual scruple he felt he could only do this if he knew the original language, just as he had learnt a considerable amount of Hebrew for the Dead Sea Scrolls book. Wilson was a man with a formidable appetite for difficulty, in fact, and I think we should all realize our debt to him by doing much more homework ourselves, for he was impatient with slovenliness. There are very few writers nowadays with this appetite for adventure and difficulty, this feeling that it is their job to bring to the English-speaking reader foreign literatures not otherwise accessible to him. Edmund Wilson was indeed one of the great messengers of culture.

Dr Leavis and the drift of civilization

PHILIP FRENCH: Frank Raymond Leavis was born in Cambridge on 14 July 1895, and except during World War I – in which he served as a non-combatant on the Western Front – he has spent his whole life there. His father was of French Huguenot stock, a man of Rationalist and Republican sympathies, who ran a small business in the town. Leavis was educated locally at the Perse School; after World War I he was a scholar at Emmanuel College, where he studied first for the historical tripos examination, then for the English tripos. Subsequently he became a university teacher, as a Fellow of Downing College from 1936 to the mid-sixties, as a university lecturer, and very late in his career as a Reader in English. It was from Cambridge that he edited his quarterly magazine *Scrutiny*. Yet while scarcely moving outside the town he has excited violent partisanship and has been one of the most influential and controversial figures of his day – as a critic, an editor, a polemicist and, supremely, as a teacher, in the very broadest sense of the term.

One of his earliest pupils was M. C. Bradbrook, Mistress of Girton 1968–76, who was taught by him in 1927 during her undergraduate days, when he was supervising English classes at Girton.

MURIEL C. BRADBROOK: Leavis seems to me to be pre-eminently a teacher. He has great charisma and always made a strong impression on his students, many of whom became life-long disciples – not a word he would like, incidentally. His power as a teacher was considerable, depending to a large extent on his own personality. The Cambridge of that time was a very exciting place, full of young poets, with William Empson as our bright particular star. It cannot happen very often that undergraduates are taught poetry written by a fellow undergraduate, but in fact we were taught about some of Empson's poems by

Leavis: I remember his reading them to us and commenting on them.

FRENCH: Muriel Bradbrook's opinion is more than
endorsed by Professor D. W. Harding, who shared Leavis
tutorials (or supervisions as they're called at Cambridge)
with another Emmanuel College undergraduate fifty years
ago, in 1925.

DENYS W. HARDING: Leavis was really superb. I remember well the feelings with which my fellow-student and I
would come away. We would be partly exhilarated, partly
somewhat subdued and rueful perhaps – exhilarated by
the fresh insights he gave us, the fine discriminations he
made and the new vistas he opened up; sobered because
his standards of insight were extremely high, making us
realize just how unskilled we ourselves were as readers,
how ignorant and immature in general (we'd come
straight from sixth-form English in a grammar school). Yet
in spite of this ruefulness there was absolutely no feeling
of belittlement. Leavis was extraordinarily understanding:
if you had difficulties or raised objections then he was
ready to meet you at once, thinking things out and discussing them just as they arose. There was nothing in the
least rigid about his teaching: he had prepared of course,
but he was always willing to scrap what he had intended
to say for the sake of whatever you might be interested
in.

FRENCH: Denys Harding went on to be a co-editor of
Scrutiny and Professor of Psychology at the University of
London. A later Leavis pupil, this time at Downing College in the 1930s, was William Walsh, who is now Professor of Commonwealth Literature and Head of the School
of English at the University of Leeds. He looks back with
equal enthusiasm to the formative influence of F. R.
Leavis's teaching.

WILLIAM WALSH: He was quite extraordinary as a
teacher. Dennis Enright has said that Leavis was one of
the few teachers he had met who treated one absolutely
as an equal, and this was indeed the case. Conversation
took place as between equals, although this assumption

of equality could sometimes be acutely embarrassing to the pupil. Leavis himself was always intensely interested in the particular piece under discussion: he observed the classical notion of the university, embodying the Socratic idea that the only authority which counted was that of the teacher over the taught. He was also a most attractive teacher, very witty and amusing, having about him a kind of well-scrubbed and athletic elegance which I, like many others, found extremely appealing. Coupled with this physical attractiveness went a startling electric quality of mind. Leavis was a man of astonishing vitality, and this vitality of being was accompanied by a great intellectual energy. One always had the feeling that one wasn't simply discussing what was there on the page. This was taking place, of course, but the discussion was deeply rooted and far-reaching, dealing with all that one felt was really important in life as a whole and in one's personal emotions and values. At that stage, after all, most undergraduates are working towards their future and developing their own particular mentality, and Leavis's teaching always seemed to engage both these facets: one's personal life, and the life of the mind – the search for the significance of life itself.

FRENCH: I have only once set eyes upon Leavis myself – when he came to address the Oxford University Critical Society in the mid-fifties – but he made an unforgettable impression. He was short and wiry, his grey hair bushy, his bald head deeply tanned, the tan reaching down to the chest that was revealed by the customary open-necked shirt. He spoke in a level, slightly nasal voice, with formidable assurance and a dry, biting wit. Here is an example: a few characteristic minutes from a lecture he gave in 1968 at the Cheltenham Literary Festival on the subject of 'T. S. Eliot and the life of English literature'. What he has to say here is central to his prophetic and social writings.

By the close of the seventeenth century the conditions of Shakespeare's kind of greatness had vanished for good. Shakespeare could be at one and the same time a supreme Renaissance poet, the highbrow poet, and draw as nobody else has ever done on the resources of

human experience, the diverse continuities behind and
implicit in the rich and robustly creative vernacular. By
1700 a transformation as momentous as any associated
with the development of modern civilization had taken
place – never to be reversed. The new Augustan culture
represented by the poetry of Pope and the prose of the
Tatler and the *Spectator* entailed an unprecedented insu-
lation of the sophisticated, the polite from the popular.
There could be no reversal. The Industrial Revolution,
which by the end of the eighteenth century was well-
advanced, worked and went on working inevitable destruction upon the inherited civilization of the people.
Dickens was the last great writer to enjoy anything of
the Shakespearean advantage. There will never be
another Dickens. What has been achieved in our time
is the complete destruction, the completion of the destruction, of that general diffused creativity which main-
tains the life, has in the past maintained the life and
continuity of a culture. For the industrial masses their
work has no human meaning in itself and offers no
satisfying interest. They save their living for their lei-
sure, of which they have very much more than their
predecessors of the Dickensian world had, but don't
know how to use it except inertly before the telly, and
in the car and the bingo hall, filling pools forms, spending money, eating fish and chips in Spain. The civilization that has disinherited them culturally and
incapacitated them humanly does nothing to give significance or any glimpse of it to their lives, or to any
lives. Significance is a profound human need, like creativity, its associate. The thwarting of the need or hunger
has consequences not the less catastrophic because of
the general blankness in face of the cause. The compla-
cent understanding with which the enlightened contemplate these things is not understanding or
enlightenment but merely a manifestation of the disease
from which our civilization is perishing. When the new
maturity acclaimed by the youth club leaders for today's
young has established its right to act out its intuitive
new wisdom independent of any derived from past
human experience, the achievement of happiness won't

really have been advanced, however confident the expectation. I have no doubt that my account of the drive of technologico-Benthamite civilization has sounded the reverse of exalted or hopeful, but if pessimism means inert acquiescence I'm certainly not a pessimist. If I was a pessimist I shouldn't be addressing a festival of literature in England as if I thought it might listen seriously to a discussion of English literature as a reality, a possible living power in our world. Actually I'm convinced that there is something to be done, that there is a sustained effort to be made, that those capable of thought and responsibility must promote in every way open to them.

FRENCH: That was F. R. Leavis himself, and there I think you have a trace of his contentious tone. He has certainly managed to get on a lot of people's nerves over the years, though so far in this programme we've only touched on the gentle side of his nature that he showed towards his pupils. I asked an admirer, the poet, critic and former Professor of Poetry at Oxford, Roy Fuller, about this other aspect of the man.

ROY FULLER: There are obviously a great number of reasons why Leavis gets on people's wick. My own feeling about the strongest part of his opposition-rousing character would be the intense seriousness with which he takes literature and creativity. Many writers and many critics, however serious they may be, have a kind of cosy side to their nature, I think: at certain points in their criticism and their creation they're inclined to drop their standards or their arduous view of life and say: 'Well, after all, things aren't so bad', 'We don't mind old Buggins or old Juggins', and so on. Leavis has never done this: probably the very notion of having some kind of programme to commemorate his eightieth birthday would not appeal to him at all, and this resistance to the cosy doesn't accord with most people's notion of what is tolerable in life. Again, in the C. P. Snow controversy he would never have acknowledged what is, I think, indubitable – Snow's own, very dignified part in what occurred. You can say what you like about C. P. Snow as a novelist, a part-time politician or a purveyor of social ideas, but his personal behaviour, his way of conducting arguments throughout, have been extremely restrained and fair-minded, it seems to me. Most of us, I think, would have been prepared to relent at some stage and say: 'Well, we don't agree with Snow but after all he is a very decent chap.' Leavis, however, would never say anything like that, because he feels that ideas are much more important than personalities. He's absolutely anti-cosy, and this is what people don't like.

FRENCH: Roy Fuller was referring there, of course, to one of the most celebrated or notorious incidents in Dr Leavis's career: his 1962 Richmond Lecture, when he attacked C. P. Snow's 'two cultures' thesis in what many considered too personal a fashion. But one doesn't necess-arily have to be a partisan of Snow to be critical of Leavis, and before going further into that controversy and into the central philosophy of Leavis's writings, here's a com-ment from John Gross, editor of the *Times Literary Supple-ment*, who was outspokenly critical of Leavis in his book *The Rise and Fall of the Man of Letters*.

JOHN GROSS: My strongest reservations would be about Leavis in the role of teacher, using that term loosely to describe someone who has followers and disciples, and whose whole approach and technique are calculated to evoke discipledom. I think myself that he's narrow, that much of what he says is arid, that he's very often an all-or-nothing man. Also, it seems to me that when he doesn't particularly respond to qualities he tends to assume they're not there, or that they're not worth paying attention to. He doesn't examine his own position, he changes his mind without drawing the proper implication – the dogmas change but not the dogmatism. But you could say this of many critics and writers: it only becomes a problem in terms of the claims made for Leavis as a central figure – claims absolutely implicit, sometimes vir-tually explicit, in his own work.

FRENCH: Well, there'll be some considerable claims made for Leavis in this programme. Let's try and pin down precisely what kind of critic he is, before going any further. I asked Christoper Ricks, Professor of English at Bristol University, to describe the tradition to which Leavis belongs.

CHRISTOPHER RICKS: Leavis belongs to the tradition which holds that there is no distinction between literary values and moral and spiritual values; hence he is at one with Dr Johnson, Matthew Arnold and T. S. Eliot in believing that aesthetic values, or literary values, should not be put into a separate category, since the reasons why we value poems are the same as those by which we evaluate people's behaviour, the state of a society or the state of an individual's consciousness. Thus it's part of Leavis's position that we shouldn't make facile distinctions between being a prophet or polemicist on the one hand, and being a critic on the other. He believes, with Arnold again, that literature represents the best that's been known and thought in the world; that literature exists because of consensuses of opinion, amounting to very important agreements about human truth and human wisdom, such as are embodied in a language, and therefore in its literature, which represents that language at its most effective, most vital and most enduring. On the other hand I think it's true that as a polemicist or prophet Leavis necessarily becomes repetitive, which doesn't apply to him as a critic; therefore I tend to return to his works of almost pure criticism, while he himself perhaps comes back to rewriting again and again his works of polemic so that they still seem as urgent in the 1970s as they were in 1960 and in 1930.

FRENCH: This question of the tradition in which Leavis belongs inevitably came up when I discussed with William Walsh one of the dominant themes running through Leavis's writings – the role of the university and of the English school within it, dealt with in such books as *Education and the University* in 1943, and more recently in *English Literature in Our Time and the University*.

WALSH: In my opinion, Leavis belongs to a critical line originating in modern times with Coleridge and Arnold

and continuing through Leavis, which seems to me to be
the grand line of the English critical tradition. These critics
all became increasingly conscious of the growing fracture
in our civilization between environment and culture; that
during the 19th and 20th century we were beginning to
live in a promiscuous world, one in which there was no
organ of authority – of inward, spiritual authority, I mean.
Coleridge, of course, thought that such an organ could be
supplied by the Church, the clerical and learned class,
while Arnold looked to the Academy, deriving this notion
from France. It seems to me that if you combine the concept of the Church, of some bruited institution, as it were,
with Arnold's idea of a source of authority which will
attempt to keep alive what is worthwhile in the tradition,
you get the general picture of why Leavis thinks that the
sole institution capable of doing this in modern society is
the university. Furthermore, within the university he saw
a very peculiar and particular role for the school of
English, for a variety of reasons.

Leavis has always taken his stand, as I see it, on both
a negative and a positive set of feelings, maintaining on
the one hand that we live in a society which is suffering
a discontinuity of consciousness with the past, while
upholding on the other his profound view of civilization
as a collaborative thing: a collaboration not simply among
the living but between the living and the dead. It follows
therefore that we are spiritually, intellectually and morally
in the position of Rousseauistically trying to recreate
individually at every given moment that which is worth
living by, which is of course impossible. Thus you have
to have an institution which persists; and within that
institution Leavis finds the most central and continuing
part of our civilization in its language. Here, after all, is
a great model of continuity, and of tradition in Lawrence's
sense – a tradition which is alive and constantly changing,
not simply a convention which is static and frozen – while
within the language he finds in its literature the concentrated model, the centre, the humanity of the tradition.
In a sense, therefore, there would seem to be a clear and
irrefragable logic in his making such a claim for literature,
which is, I know, frequently scoffed at by others, even

arts people, who ask, 'Why literature'? To which I would reply: because literature is language supremely charged and worthwhile and shaped; because it is both instinctive and discursive; because it's that which, as Coleridge says, provides a second nature for man. This seems to me a marvellously clear and logical position; even though you may not accept it, finding it too great a claim perhaps, I don't think it can be attacked on the grounds of logic or prejudice.

Remember also that Leavis is profoundly anti-academic in the traditional sense, that he has a horror of the inert and the encapsulated, the non-living quality of so much academic life and discourse. I suppose it may well be that some of his criticism of universities, and of Cambridge in particular, comes from his own personal experience; but surely anyone who has lived in universities must know that they have a disposition to become crystallized. He struck us, as pupils (and his work indeed bears this out), both as a person profoundly convinced of the importance of the continuity of the human mind, of human experience, and as someone extremely revolutionary in his dissatisfaction with the current and fashionable expositions of this belief. For example, I think one of the reasons for his attack on the Bloomsbury group lies in the fact that it was a current fashionable crystallization, out of touch with the past and looking in upon itself. Leavis has always had an extraordinary civic sense of the obligations of the teacher and of the university: the claims he puts forward for the university and for the English school carry with them immense obligations to the society outside. They're not a claim for some sort of mandarin status; on the contrary, they are more of a claim to be the servants of the servants of God – quite a different emphasis.

FRENCH: Those are the views of William Walsh, who is incidentally currently engaged in writing a book about Dr Leavis. As he suggested, the question naturally arises as to whether English literature and English studies can bear the particular burden that Leavis imposes on them. I put this question to Christopher Ricks.

RICKS: There is an important difference, I think, between

claims which might be made for English literature on the one hand and for English study on the other. From my point of view it seems true to say that the literature of a country must be able to embody the profoundest knowledge of what that country is about. Literature exists in the very medium which we use all the time to communicate with each other. It is therefore in a special position, in comparison with the other arts – not more important, but unique. It's uniquely English in a way in which English painting, the Englishness of other English arts, is not. A lot of people who object to Leavis's claims for English studies are really objecting to his claims for the value of literature. Though many people say they're disputing the one, they are really concerned with the other. I believe Leavis deeply deplores the fact that English studies now have to carry so much of the responsibility for the survival of English literature. He cannot suppose what's happened by way of the decay of a general reading public to be desirable; indeed it's very clear from his own writing, and from that of Mrs Leavis, that he considers this disastrous. If the survival of English literature is not to depend on English studies, however, it's not clear to me where its preservation lies; though I can see that it amounts to a problem and an anxiety for many people in the field of literary studies that Leavis does seem at times to underrate the humanizing power, vitality and intelligence of some of the other humane disciplines, such as history and philosophy.

FRENCH: We've discussed the placing of Dr Leavis in an English tradition, but in contemporary terms, just what kind of critic is he? Here's the view of George Steiner, Extraordinary Fellow of Churchill College, Cambridge, and now Professor of English and Comparative Literature at the University of Geneva.

STEINER: We should distinguish, I think, between different kinds of critics. There are those whose writings are themselves almost a parallel to the work they're talking about. They are writer-critics, who sometimes create in their essay or book of criticism almost a challenge to the poem or novel or drama which they're discussing. G.

Wilson Knight would be my leading example here. Then there are analysts of literature who are primarily concerned with philosophy or linguistics, who study the poem or the novel in question as an example – a supremely privileged one, of course, but still an example – of how we relate word to meaning or language to reality: I'm thinking here of I. A. Richards and William Empson. There are also critics who may be poets themselves – the American New Critics, John Crowe Ransom, R. P. Blackmur, Allen Tate – who try to take us inside the workshop. How does the poem get built? And we read them with interest because they are poets themselves. Again, there are critics who think my job – my difficult job, at the risk of getting a lot of things wrong – is to tell the reader what is going on today, what writers he should read, who is important, who is ephemeral. These critics (and the line between the reviewer and the critic is here almost impossible to draw) would, I think, be most brilliantly represented in our century by Edmund Wilson.

Leavis does not belong readily to any of these categories. I imagine only his most fanatical and devoted followers take any pleasure in his prose style, while Leavis himself regards with trenchant disapproval, great irony in fact, those who try to make of their criticism a lyric counterpart to the work they're talking about. He finds them self-advertising and vulgar. Leavis is certainly not a theoretician of language or of literary form. There's a famous exchange with the American scholar René Wellek in which he said: 'I don't want to be a philosophic critic in that sense of the word, in that use of philosophy.' He has said more recently that modern linguistics has nothing real to bring to the judgment of a work of literature. He's not very interested in the genesis of the work; you'd never find a Leavis essay based on the successive drafts of a poem, such as often happens with the New Critics. His judgments of contemporaries have, with very few exceptions, been eccentric and usually irritated; it would be utterly invidious to name the one modern novelist or the one modern poet whom he has strongly backed, both being now essentially forgotten. Nevertheless his achievement is, I'm certain, of absolutely central importance.

If I had to define him, I would say that Leavis is a complete reader of the rarest and most necessary kind. I mean something like this: confronted by the page, he reads with a scruple, with a totality of attention and with such informing power, keeping detail accurately balanced in proportion to the work as a whole, that he elicits from himself, and from all those readers whom he invites to collaborate with him, a response which is also in a full sense responsibility – responsibility, that is, towards literature, towards language, towards the conditions of political society and of education, in which literature can be a humane, shaping force, a discipline which makes our feelings richer and more exact. Leavis's literary criticism and his teaching – they're totally the same – are part of the absolute integrity of the man. There's no difference between Leavis the writer of a book and Leavis in a tutorial or lecture. This unity is a constant and central act of reading. I think we're at a moment when serious reading, the attempt to relate text to the whole of social and political context, is being eroded to such a point that it threatens to become a specialized university technique. Leavis's role has been crucial. Whether or not we agree with his choice of canonic books – and I don't think we need to – whether or not we accept his specific judgment of what he's reading – and many of these judgments, that on Shelley, for example, seem to me vehemently myopic – simply doesn't matter. All of us who try to read well, giving ourselves and opening our minds to a writer in order to answer him responsibly, all of us who try to read with others – and my conception of the teaching of literature is just this – remain very formidably in his debt.

FRENCH: Leavis's quarterly magazine *Scrutiny* took its title from a series of articles in the *Calendar of Modern Letters*, a short-lived critical journal of the 1920s edited by Edgell Rickword, that Leavis greatly admired. (In 1933 Leavis edited and introduced *Towards Standards of Criticism: Selections from the Calendar of Modern Letters*.) *Scrutiny* was largely a literary journal, but not entirely so. It carried articles on psychology, for instance, and on music (mostly by Leavis's former pupil and one-time co-editor, the

musicologist Wilfrid Mellers), together with a great deal
of material on problems of culture and education. In its
first number, in May 1932, the editors proclaimed that 'a
review is necessary that combines criticism of literature
with criticism of extra-literary activities. We take it as axio-
matic that concern for standards of living implies concern
for standards in the arts'. One of the contributors to the
first *Scrutiny*, and one of its editors from 1933–47, was
Denys Harding; I asked about the magazine's aims, and
how they had changed over the years.

HARDING: I wouldn't say that *Scrutiny*'s aims did change
very much really. The purpose was always to provide the
opportunity for people to think about literature seriously
and then to discuss it from the point of view of the highest
standards that they could achieve, looking on it not as a
specialism, not as something with which the English
teacher at a university or the narrow English scholar alone
was concerned, but stressing always the relevance of literature to one's personal values, the ongoing development between one's reading and understanding of
literature and one's own personality, including of course
one's personal outlook on social affairs.

FRENCH: Another of the contributors to the first *Scrutiny*
was Muriel Bradbrook. She spoke to me about the magazine's close relationship to the Cambridge English tripos
of that time, which she described as a very daring and
innovatory programme in its day, and one much copied
around the world.

BRADBROOK: I would say this new approach consisted
of a concern with contemporary literature and with judg-
ing literature – with what Leavis called 'Discrimination'.
The regular treatment of English literature with strings of
dates (the work of Oliver Elton or Legouis-Cazamian, for
instance, illustrated by the *Cambridge History of English
Literature*) had been annalistic, leading you through from
the beginning to the end; and this view had been
defended. For example, my friend C. S. Lewis upheld it
passionately, maintaining that this was the only way to
teach the subject. Leavis took an entirely different view,

like a good many people in Cambridge, particularly Richards, namely that one should read literature in order to distinguish the first-rate from the second-rate, the authentic from the bogus. Leavis's innovation, as compared with the work done by Richards, was that he had himself worked within the English tripos, under its old, unreformed shape of course, and had taken a PhD (on the *Tatler* and *Spectator*). Moreover he had a strong historical sense of English literature, therefore his attitude was not just the result of the kind of preference for shopping around which you find in modern schools of English literature. This would not suit him at all, as his last book, *Nor Shall My Sword*, makes perfectly clear.

FRENCH: In the bibliography of his book *Culture and Environment* (1933), Dr Leavis described *Scrutiny* thus: 'A quarterly review intended to keep those concerned about the drift of civilization (and especially those in the schools) in touch with literature and the movement of ideas.' The journal was not the product of a clique of Leavisites as has often been claimed, or even of English teachers. In fact in the twenty-one years that it ran, 1932–53, there were around 150 contributors. Among them incidentally were Norman Podhoretz, now editor of the American magazine *Commentary*, and Wolf Mankowitz, who both published their first essays in *Scrutiny* while still students at Cambridge.

During the 1930s *Scrutiny* sold 750 copies a quarter; this had doubled by the 1950s, and such had been the demand for copies after it ceased publication that in 1963 the whole thing was reprinted in twenty volumes. In his fine collection of essays, *Experience into Words*, D. W. Harding has included a number of pieces he wrote for *Scrutiny*; in the introduction he thanks Dr Leavis for his encouragement and refers to his having kept *Scrutiny* going 'in face of great difficulties and intense hostility'. I asked Professor Harding to tell me about those difficulties and that hostility.

HARDING: As to the hostility he met with, Leavis's general situation in Cambridge must be quite well-known: although he was on the fringe of English teaching all the

time, with some supervision always and later some lec-
turing, he wasn't accepted by the English school at all
happily. Leavis's own feeling was certainly that they
wanted to get rid of him, to squeeze him out or tempt
him away, perhaps, to some remote part of the Commonwealth; but he was determined to remain in Cambridge,
because he felt that by being there he would have students
of the quality he valued, whom he could teach at the level
that he was interested in. Leavis was ostracized to a large
extent by people in the English school, though not by all
of them. There were some who always kept in touch with
him, I believe, but they were far more closely connected
with other members of the faculty who would have
nothing whatever to do with him.

The difficulties Leavis had to contend with were largely
the financial problems of keeping *Scrutiny* going. The
work was entirely voluntary: there was no payment for
contributors, and certainly none for editors. We were all
of us having to earn our living in other ways. The printer
had to be paid, the distributors too, and it was very much
a hand-to-mouth affair. There was a time, as I recall, when
Leavis even wrote round to the rest of us on the editorial
board saying that he would be grateful if we could contribute a little towards the postal costs; the money coming
in wasn't really covering his expenses, and of course he
was hard up himself. I remember I managed to scrape up
£2, out of a salary of £250 in my first university post. This
was how *Scrutiny* was run; we really were in very great
difficulties all the time.

The other problem which Leavis had to face constantly
was that of getting contributions of the quality he wanted.
In fact, each issue more or less amounted to a crisis, as he
was never sure until the last moment whether there would
be enough to fill it. Often, of course, he himself had to
write for an issue very much more, and much faster, than
he'd intended. Indeed, the whole matter was an enormous burden, of which naturally he bore the main part,
and for so long.

FRENCH: F. R. Leavis has the reputation of being a very
difficult man, and it would be misleading not to confront

this; therefore I went on to ask Professor Harding to what extent Dr Leavis's conflict with the Cambridge academic establishment was due to his views, and to what extent it stemmed from his personality.

HARDING: The two things go together, I think, because of his strong feeling that English literature was a serious study which couldn't be set apart as a specialism in the way that the scientist, perhaps, can isolate his work from the rest of his life. Leavis always held that literature and individual judgments about literature constituted a very important expression of individual personality; so that if he found your judgments insensitive or stupid, dishonest or conventional, he was inevitably making a criticism of your personality. If he thought that while your views were highly scholarly in one direction you were also being trivial in admiring P. G. Wodehouse, for instance, he would say so and indicate his disapproval. This meant inevitably that he came up against some of the more conventional people who were teaching English in those days. If his personality had been different – more like mine – he would certainly not have stood out with such courage and defiance; I've always gone for protective coloration but he would never compromise. There was this interaction between his high standards and his view of those standards as reflections of something greater than a merely specialist job, which led to his absolute refusal to compromise.

FRENCH: Much of Dr Leavis's finest writing is to be found in *Scrutiny*, but his first major critical work, *New Bearings in English Poetry*, was published the year the magazine started; his major work on Dickens, written in collaboration with his wife, Q. D. Leavis, came out in 1970, and all but one chapter is the product of the post-*Scrutiny* years. It is claimed that his criticism has changed the way we look at English literature; so to get a statement of both the orthodox view of his achievement, and a critique of it, I turned to John Gross.

GROSS: Has Leavis indeed recharted the course of English literature for readers and students? Even to begin to

answer that question is in some way to take him at his
own evaluation, which is certainly not mine. I don't
believe literature works as he sees it, nor that his influence
on writers and readers has been as great as the question
implies. On students – yes, up to a point: in so far as he
has recharted the course it has been much more in education. But even so, even if people believe it to be so,
what has he actually done?

To my mind, Leavis's achievement has several phases,
according to which part of his career you are talking about;
very roughly, simplifying rather brutally, I would say that
initially, in the first phase of his career (the period of *New
Bearings in English Poetry*) he sought to establish within an
academic context that there had been a literary revolution
in the 1920s, associated above all with T. S. Eliot and
Pound, with the discovery of Gerard Manley Hopkins,
and so forth. From this he tried to draw certain conclusions for the study of English poetry (poetry being his
main interest at that period). He worked backwards, looking for qualities of metaphysical wit that Eliot himself, for
example, had already found, going to the obvious place
in Donne. These were the kind of qualities Leavis went
for – complexity, a certain form of dramatic re-enactment
within language – and this pursuit involved, again speaking very loosely, a rejection of the romantic, the diluted
and rather deliquescent pattern of conventional teaching
of English – Eng Lit if you like – at that stage. He also
concentrated, notoriously, on close reading, on trying to
get people to look at what the words were actually doing:
sometimes indeed, in his writing, he does demonstrate
under a magnifying glass the way verbal effects are
brought about in poetry. With this, of course, there go a
set of revaluations of individual figures, some being
brought forward and some downgraded: like Milton or
more drastically Shelley, to take glaring examples. Even
where he accepts valuations, sometimes it's not simply a
question of upgrading: Pope, for instance, had been
brought forward in the 1920s by Bloomsbury to some
extent, though Leavis went on to make a more plausible
and more interesting case for Pope, I think, perceiving his

affinities with Marvell, Donne or other seventeenth-century predecessors, among other insights.

That gives some account of the first phase of Leavis's career. Later on there came a shift of emphasis towards the novel. The most celebrated embodiment of this (though he modified it subsequently) lies in his book *The Great Tradition*, which brings forward Jane Austen, albeit off-stage, George Eliot, more unexpectedly than any other of the figures, Joseph Conrad, Henry James, to the centre of the stage, and, increasingly, D. H. Lawrence. This is not just a shift from one genre to another, in my view: it involves the replacement of Eliot by Lawrence at the centre of Leavis's critical universe, which in turn implies less emphasis on close reading. Even though he would say, and his admirers with him, that he looks for the poetic qualities, patternings and local verbal effects in fiction, yet fiction only lends itself to such treatment up to a certain point. This shift of emphasis led to the concentration on moral and social criticism which Leavis had already voiced early on in books like *Culture and Environment*, but which had not run in tandem with his earlier writing on poetry, as I see it. His social critique becomes more central now that he's discussing the novel and novelists; and he's gone on changing his mind, though not always acknowledging to what extent Dickens, who was on the whole treated very marginally in *The Great Tradition*, becomes another central preoccupation later on.

FRENCH: That is an outline of the paths along which Dr Leavis's literary criticism has developed and of how it has reshaped the way we look at the course of English literature. As John Gross has suggested, one could argue that the polemical or prophetic role has become increasingly important in his work, though it was always there, of course. One can find it expressed with great urgency in the book he wrote with Denys Thompson forty years ago, *Cutlure and Environment* – a book incidentally that has remained in print, selling steadily over the years. It has been used to train successive generations of schoolchildren and students in how to understand and to resist the blandishments of advertisers and the seductive rhetoric of mass communicators. It was the book through which I, as a schoolboy, together with many others, first came into contact with Leavis's work. In *Culture and Environment*, he wrote:

> We cannot, as we might in a healthy state of culture, leave the citizen to be formed unconsciously by the environment; if anything like a worthy idea of satisfactory living is to be saved, he must be trained to discriminate and resist.

I asked Christopher Ricks if there was any basis for thinking that Leavis the prophet or polemicist had been gaining ascendancy over Leavis the critic.

RICKS: I think it is true to say that lately Leavis has been necessarily much more concerned with the whole state of civilization. After all, Lawrence is no longer alive; and whatever the hypothetical answer may be as to how he and Leavis would have got on, the fact remains that as long as Lawrence was alive – Eliot also, up to the date of his *Four Quartets*, let's say – Leavis could feel that there were great writers in existence offering profound critiques of the way we live, of modern urban industrial civilization. He no longer believes (and I agree with him) that such writers do exist; therefore their roles devolve upon the critic and the university, which is a great pity. It would be far better if we did not have to look on the universities as the only real guardians now of our literary tradition; and this certainly wasn't true in Victorian England.

FRENCH: There is another aspect to Dr Leavis's writing on culture, and that is the way in which he has influenced the fairly recent study of popular culture and mass communications. Stuart Hall is the director of the Centre for Contemporary Cultural Studies at Birmingham University, and co-author of *The Popular Arts*: I asked him about the contribution of Dr and Mrs Leavis to our thinking about cultural questions and popular culture.

STUART HALL: In the first place although they have both been very sensitive throughout their work to the way in which developed literary forms have popular idioms of

expression and feeling behind them, I think it is true to
say that in fact F. R. Leavis hasn't written a great deal
about popular culture himself. That aspect is very much
more associated with Mrs Leavis's early book, *Fiction and
the Reading Public*, which was a very important book in its
time and has remained so ever since. Therefore I would
not say that their influence in terms of popular culture is
based on a sustained body of work; in my view it has
more to do with the fact that at a certain point in the
twenties and thirties they did raise central questions con-
cerning the nature and direction of English culture. This
must have been just about the time when Britain became
a kind of mass culture, a mass society. I'm thinking spe-
cifically about the pamphlet *Mass Civilization and Minority
Culture*, and Leavis's book *Culture and Environment*, which
in a sense initiated a whole school of cultural criticism.
That seems to me their most important activity – just
putting those questions on the agenda and saying in a
phrase that anybody who is seriously concerned about
the society and the fate of literature has to be concerned
about the whole range of cultural questions.

The second point is, of course, that people learnt a great
deal from their literary practice. If you think of the work
of Richard Hoggart and Raymond Williams, for instance,
or of my own Centre in its early stages, I should say we
were influenced not precisely by the essays which the
Leavises had produced but rather by borrowing a method
they had applied to the study of serious literature, as well
as to popular forms: popular fiction, films and so on. The
nub of the Leavises' influence here, surely, was their
insistence that rather than drifting away from the film or
novel you were discussing to large questions about the
culture in general, you should instead give close attention
to the forms and the language themselves. You had to be
specific and concrete, and in so far as people made a sort
of Leavisite practice of popular cultural criticism it was by
attending to popular cultural forms seriously, in their con-
creteness and specificity. This seems to me another influence, though a secondary one.

The third point I would make is that looking back now
on the whole work of the Leavises and of *Scrutiny* from

the thirties onward one can see, more clearly in retrospect perhaps than one could at the time, that this was very firmly rooted in a certain cultural model, a conservative cultural model. From these roots came the notion about training in discrimination, that this was a complex thing to which only a few common readers could aspire, that cultural civilized standards would have to be defended by a minority, and so on. All this, which seems to emerge more in popular awareness in relation to Leavis's work in the forties and fifties, was really there from the very beginning. He has been quite consistent about it. There are many people concerned with popular culture who take quite the opposite view and use quite a different cultural model, and are therefore not influenced by the Leavises' work, but who nevertheless respect the presence of that conservative model, as I certainly do myself. It is a tough, serious attitude: I think it is fundamentally in error, but it is with some relief that one finds in England a cultural criticism so firmly rooted in a conservative tradition. It is not so often that one does; and this constitutes a force of opposition in the field, as it were, rather than an influence.

FRENCH: Conservative his position may well be, but Dr Leavis has never taken a political turn to left or right, though he has admitted to voting for the Liberal Party.

Stuart Hall was talking there very much in terms of the Leavises' joint achievement, and in speaking to Professor Bradbrook I raised the question as to how important had been the role and contribution of Queenie Leavis to her husband's work.

BRADBROOK: I think she contributed a tremendous amount, giving him a great sense of confidence and enterprise. They married in 1929; before that Leavis had not published anything, though he must have been thirty-four, but within a couple of years of their marriage he had published three books. The powerfulness of Queenie Leavis's mind, her precocity and brilliance, have had a notable effect, certainly. Husband and wife were in every sense partners in *Scrutiny*; it was their joint enterprise, and I'm sure other people like Professor Harding and

Professor Knights would agree that although their names also were on the cover it was really the Leavises who did all the donkey-work, together, for the production of the magazine.

FRENCH: You would ascribe quite a considerable importance to Queenie Leavis's *Fiction and the Reading Public*?

BRADBROOK: Yes, I think so. This was her PhD thesis and it was definitely an innovatory work. You can see the influence of that approach in Leavis's work also, I believe, for they mutually influenced each other. He had taught her as an undergraduate, of course, when she was at Girton. It seems to me that Leavis's sense of the importance of the novel, bringing it out as the predominant literary form in the nineteenth century, represents a radical shift of appreciation on his part in regard to that period, which is still not universally acknowledged, though widely recognized.

FRENCH: Earlier in the programme George Steiner referred rather dismissively to Dr Leavis's own literary style, but his view is not universally shared. True, R. H. S. Crossman remarked that 'what was once his abject failure to write decent English has become the mannerism of a famous man'. On the other hand, Denis Donoghue has observed that 'at his best he is a powerful writer, and the elaborate deployment of qualifications, interjections, and parentheses has the effect of entangling the reader in a network of implication: he will not be released until the sentence is complete.' Another admirer of Dr Leavis's style is Christopher Ricks.

RICKS: As with all strongly idiosyncratic and personal writers, his manner necessarily becomes mannerism at times, so that he is an easy person to quote from for derisive purposes. On the other hand he is also an extremely good writer, in my opinion. His basic intuition, if you like, was that the style of Henry James could and should be adapted to much more manly, aggressive, combative purposes than James ever realized, and that what may seem merely qualifications, nuances or asides are capable of exerting tremendous, charming and witty energy and animus. The relationship of animus/animation to animus/animosity forms part of this argument, of course; I don't see how anybody could read the beginning of, say, Leavis's essay on *The Dunciad* and not find this a wonderful way to write an English sentence. I think he's an exceptionally good writer, but as with James, Arnold, Ruskin, Carlyle – as with all the Victorian sages, in fact – his manner can become self-parody, though this seldom happens in his case, I would say.

FRENCH: Let me quote that opening sentence from *The Dunciad* essay in *The Common Pursuit*:

> Yes, one concedes grudgingly, overcoming the inevitable revulsion, as one turns the pages of this new edition (the 'Twickenham'), in which the poem trickles thinly through a desert of apparatus, to disappear time and again from sight – yes, there has to be a *Dunciad* annotated, garnished and be-prosed in this way.

Leavis's style is frequently at the service of brutal and devastating dismissals. Apart from errant authors, the targets that so often come in for his withering scorn include the BBC Third Programme (or Radio 3), the Sunday press, the *New Statesman*, the Arts Council, and other representatives of what Dr Leavis considers a frivolous metropolitan culture that inhibits the creation of a genuinely educated and responsive public. Mrs Leavis once said of the task of putting down an opponent that 'it was a duty as well as a pleasure'. I asked Professor Harding whether he thought Dr Leavis derived enjoyment from handing down his magisterial rebukes.

HARDING: I suppose everybody who has the job of criticizing – ruthlessly criticizing in fact, as Leavis often felt was necessary – must enjoy doing it well, effectively that is. Therefore the stinging phrase is as welcome to Leavis as it was to Pope, inevitably. This must be true, I think, and the target never enjoys it. There was a time, of course when not only his targets but many other people felt that he was much too ruthless; I myself came in for a certain amount of pressure from friends and acquaintances and colleagues – even, as I remember, from a student on one occasion, who thought it was dreadful that I should be associated with *Scrutiny*! She had produced some attack on somebody she liked (I can't remember who) and she was really quite upset that I should have anything to do with it.

FRENCH: The recipient of one of Leavis's most swingeing attacks was, as I've already mentioned, C. P. Snow. Like other aspects of Leavis's career, this affair is too complicated to go into in much detail here: the best examination of the subject is a lengthy essay by Lionel Trilling in *Beyond Culture*. But here are a few words on the matter by Roy Fuller.

FULLER: Leavis is against Snow, I imagine, because Snow would admit virtue in increasing material prosperity as a paramount thing. That is to say, it would be much more important for Snow that children shouldn't starve than that they should be brought up in the right moral framework. Now one doesn't want to put words into Leavis's mouth, but he would consider that the material conditions of life were far less important than the – for want of a better word – spiritual conditions. It is this kind of puritanical rigour, purveyed by Leavis in all departments of his writing and activities, which sharply differentiates him from Snow, as I see it, indeed from most other people too.

FRENCH: What Roy Fuller says of the Snow-Leavis controversy is borne out by the characteristically pessimistic remark in a letter that Dr Leavis wrote to *The Times* in 1974: 'The sickness of humanity today', he said, 'is that it has nothing to believe in but economic growth, money, equality and welfare.'

It is difficult to know just how influential these writings are today. Of course many of his ideas and judgments have become part of the general literary and cultural consensus, frequently – as Dr and Mrs Leavis have pointed out with a certain air of justified grievance – without the source being adequately acknowledged or even recognized at all. Unquestionably, the tone of criticism has become altogether more rigorous in both the academic world and in literary journalism since he entered upon the scene.

Leavis continues to have his dedicated partisans, the Leavisites, who are often said to be more royalist than the king, and he continues to enjoy the respect of a wide circle of readers. But Professor Bradbrook would place the time of his greatest influence in the years immediately after the Second World War.

BRADBROOK: I would say that his influence was at its very widest in the forties and early fifties, when *Scrutiny* was well-established, when his pupils were beginning to go out and the Downing school had formed. Leavis caught the period of expanding studies in grammar schools following the Butler Education Act; the meritocracy, which believed in rather strenuous and puritanical self-cultivation. Modern attitudes have changed considerably since then; and while Leavis has clearly been immensely popular and has enjoyed himself very much at York and the other universities he has visited after his retirement (where the students do admire him greatly), I think, as one can see from his last book, *Nor Shall My Sword*, he is not much in sympathy with modern educational developments, because of his belief in what is sometimes called 'élitism' (it is used as a boo word, as a derogation). He is quite firmly on the side of the élite, it seems to me.

FRENCH: One of the members of that post-war generation is Martin Green, who now teaches in America. In the late fifties Green wrote a key book of the period called *A Mirror for Anglo-Saxons* – an examination of British culture, partly autobiographical, in which he set up F. R. Leavis, George Orwell, Kingsley Amis and D. H. Lawrence as representative figures of British decency, of the national qualities he admired and was guided by. I asked Dr Green what it was that Leavis embodied for him.

MARTIN GREEN: Leavis stands for a number of things to me personally which are also impersonal elements in British cultural life; but it would be as true to say that he stands for just one thing. He is, or he was, the antagonist of British cultural life, the man who opposed the dominant forces, who stood out against them on behalf of other forgotten, beleaguered modes of Britishness. That is always an attractive posture, of course, and Leavis's enemies thought it was *their* posture. The dandies of the twenties believed they were standing for the forgotten and beleaguered traditions of aestheticism in England. What makes the posture belong to Leavis and not to them, in the long run, is something objective, in some sense: that is, for people like me and for the decades from 1930 to 1960 Leavis was right and they were wrong. To be more specific about his antagonism, Leavis was the puritan rebuking the hedonism of Bloomsbury and the clubs and academia, in the name of moral intensity. All these terms are really metaphors to be applied to the life of the imagination.

Leavis was also the Lawrentian rebuking the life pessimism of T. S. Eliot, and, implicitly, of modernists like Baudelaire and Kafka. Again, he was the critic who centred the imaginative life in the faculty of judgment, not of fantasy, and therefore the enemy of Edith Sitwell and Dylan Thomas. He was the manly man. Lastly, he was the man of tradition as opposed to experimentalism and modernism, though his tradition was of course very idiosyncratic, going back via Victorians like Leslie Stephen to John Bunyan and the folk life. And all the things Leavis said 'no' to, and 'yes' to, had analogues and allies in the non-intellectual forms of British life. I haven't time to go into all that now, but it constituted an important part of what made his leadership so exhilarating and inspiriting for me, and for people like me.

FRENCH: Martin Green gave a very personal reading of Leavis, though not I think a misreading, and a very favourable one. Has Leavis been widely misunderstood and misrepresented? He himself is inclined to think so, as are many of his followers.

RICKS: Leavis has often been misrepresented, I feel. To begin with, he is a very easy figure simply to make jokes about; you have only to mention his name and there follows an assumption of easy enlightened superiority to his fervour, his puritanism, and so on. But the really important misrepresentation, to my mind, is to see him above all as a negative and demolishing critic, to maintain that revaluation in his eyes consists mostly of devaluation and denigration. I don't think that's true: on the contrary, a lot of his very best criticism is in the simplest sense positive and affirmative. He writes wonderfully about why Eliot is very good, why Keats is very good even with reservations, and so on. There's a poem by Ben Jonson, *To the Learned Critic*, which seems to me to catch some of the feeling one might have if one were an artist (which I'm not) – that one would rather have small praise from somebody whose standards were not ephemeral than garlands from the easy-to-please. It goes like this:

> May others fear, fly, and traduce thy name
> As guilty men do magistrates; glad I,
> That wish my poems a legitimate fame,
> Charge them, for crown, to thy sole censure high;
> And but a sprig of bays, given by thee,
> Shall outlive garlands stolen from the chaste tree.

The 'sprig of bays' given with qualifications to Eliot, to Empson or to other living or recent writers by Leavis who is sparing with his praise seems to me worth a lot more than the easy praises of other men.

FRENCH: After that invocation of Ben Jonson, a final word from a present-day poet, Roy Fuller, who told me this, when I asked what was the very special quality that set Dr Leavis apart.

FULLER: What one finds extra in Leavis is his particular long view of poetry and the novel, together with his persistence, banging away at ideas which in the end do prove themselves to be of enormous importance, so that one is always saying to oneself 'yes, he really is right about this' – the long-term ideas which keep coming up in his critical works, such as the notion that only in the university is there sufficient disinterest to generate ideas of value, untainted by self-interest. I find this very moving. Not that Leavis is at all idealistic about the university – indeed he is often scathing about what goes on in universities and what the average academic is like. But if we were to

be condemned to another Dark Age, the Leavisian idea
that culture would repose in the universities, being kept
safe there for a new Renaissance, is deeply touching, and
may not after all be terribly wide of the mark. I believe it
is this long-term view which differentiates him essentially
from other critics. F. R. Leavis is a good Eng Lit critic,
yes, but he has his own particular set of ideas as well; and
this is what sets him apart.

Lionel Trilling, 1905–1975

PHILIP FRENCH: In Britain Lionel Trilling's reputation is high and secure, though restricted to a relatively small circle of readers. His studies of Matthew Arnold and E. M. Forster, his novel *The Middle of the Journey*, his critical essays, most notably those collected in 1950 under the title *The Liberal Imagination*, have not wanted for admirers here, and during the latter part of his life he was a welcome lecturer and visiting professor in this country. Yet for all his high standing on this side of the Atlantic he was never the controversial, emblematic, or charismatic figure that he became – and continues to be – in America. One of my aims is to explain the peculiar position he has in American intellectual life; another, connected to it, is to show why his writings and cast of mind have an enduring importance for us here as well.

Let us start with a word from Professor Morris Dickstein, one of New York's brightest younger critics: I have heard the gist of what he says variously expressed by many Americans over the years.

MORRIS DICKSTEIN: I remember very vividly reading *The Liberal Imagination* at the end of my second year at Columbia, along with Jacques Barzun's book *Teacher in America*. Now Barzun's book helped make me decide not to be a journalist but to become a university teacher: that book did its work for me and I've never looked at it again. Trilling's book really showed me what I wanted to do with my chosen career: the paperback copy that I first read in 1959 eventually became so dog-eared from reading and re-reading that it completely disintegrated.

FRENCH: Columbia University in New York, one of America's oldest, richest and most distinguished universities, was the centre of Trilling's life from his student days in the 1920s until his death in 1975, when he had become an Emeritus Professor. The historian Jacques Bar-

zun, author of the other book that determined Dickstein's
vocation, was a student contemporary of Trilling's: I asked
him how Trilling appeared to him at that time.

JACQUES BARZUN: He made rather a slight and fugitive impression on me, because during our undergraduate
years we did not move in the same college circles. I considered him something of an aesthete, a symbolist so to
speak, a very sensitive, intelligent and courteous person,
but not one with whom I would ever become friendly.
Our friendship developed a good while later, in the mid-
thirties, when he came back to Columbia after teaching in
two other colleges. We were assigned to conduct together
a seminar, more exactly a colloquium, on a series of great
books – the beginning of the 'great books' idea which was
exploited further later on by the University of Chicago.
During this colloquium we found that despite radically
different points of origin, political inclinations and literary
experience we were extremely congenial, so that we were
able to make a fairly good job of teaching our dozen or so
students; and this first happy association turned into a
lifelong friendship.

FRENCH: That seminar on the social and cultural context
of literature and ideas, conducted by Barzun and Trilling
for nearly forty years at Columbia, became something of
a legend for its rigour, intellectual elegance and high spir-
its. It was there that in a discussion on Malthusian theory
someone happened to invoke the motto of the Knights of
the Garter. 'Honi soit qui Malthus pense', said Trilling, to
which Barzun came back with 'Honi soit qui Mal Thus
puns'.

How Trilling came to be at Columbia in the first place,
and return there in the second place, is of some importance. He was born in New York City on 4 July 1905, the
son of Eastern European Jewish immigrants. His father
was a tailor and an unsuccessful businessman, who came
to America at the age of sixteen; his mother, the eldest of
eleven children, had been born in the East End of London
and also came to New York in her mid-teens. From his
self-educated mother Trilling inherited a love of English
literature: she read him Dickens and Kipling as a child,

and there was nothing but encouragement from home when the study and teaching of literature came up. But how important was his Jewish background? I put this question to the critic and literary historian Irving Howe.

IRVING HOWE: On the face of it his Jewish background did not seem terribly important, because for many people he was, let us say, the Arnoldian critic *par excellence*; and there must have been people who didn't even know that he was of Jewish extraction. It's amusing to recall that when I was researching for my book *World of our Fathers* I came across a volume dealing with the East European city of Byalistok, in which there was a section about a rather influential and affluent family called Trilling: I asked Lionel about this (it must have been about five or six years ago) and without batting an eyelid he said 'Of course, that is my family' – but this extraordinarily suave, elegant, dapper man didn't look or behave quite as if he were descended from the Byalistok Trillings. On the other hand, the Byalistok Trillings may have had a good deal more diversity than we suppose. The Jewish background *was* important, in fact: for a long period of time it was kept down, so that not many of us knew of his early involvement with the *Menorah Journal*, which was a kind of cultural Jewish magazine in the late twenties. I think that as he grew older it became more important again.

FRENCH: Only occasionally in his later writings did Trilling make more than passing reference to his Jewish background: an important instance is the essay 'Wordsworth and the Rabbis', in his book *The Opposing Self*. But there is a little-known memoir, published as an afterword to a reissue of Tess Slesinger's novel *The Unpossessed*, in which he recalls the stories and essays on Jewish themes that he wrote for the *Menorah Journal* from his undergraduate days up to 1930. 'We were not religious . . . it had nothing to do with Zionism', he wrote. 'Chiefly our concern with Jewishness was about what is now called authenticity.' That is a key word in Trilling's later writing – authenticity – contrasted with sincerity in his final masterpiece of intellectual history *Sincerity and Authenticity*. His former Columbia pupil (in the thirties) and later faculty colleague

Quentin Anderson sees the exploration of the meaning of Jewish life as a phase in the young Trilling's development.

QUENTIN ANDERSON: As a young man, of course, he had written for the *Menorah Journal*, which was in large part devoted to the exploration of the meaning of Jewishness in American life. I think he felt that having examined this he did not need to go on to plunge into the Philip Roth kind of investigation of the matter. His aim was to join the company of those who would take Jewishness for granted, in some way, among other looming cultural facts.

FRENCH: Nevertheless in the 1920s, when he went off to teach in the Middle West for a year and then spent some eight years back in New York at Hunter College, his Jewishness was at issue in his career, as Irving Howe explains.

HOWE: He told me – and this is no secret – that when he finished his doctoral work at Columbia (and he surely must have been its most brilliant student of English in fifty or sixty years) some stuffy old professor told him that he did not have much of a future in the profession as a teacher of English literature because he wasn't, as a Jew, sufficiently attuned to the Anglo-Saxon spirit! He was let go at Columbia and went, I believe, to the University of Wisconsin for a year or two, after which Columbia had enough sense to bring him back. I would guess – it is no more than a guess – that this was for him a fairly critical, perhaps even traumatic incident, since in conversation he would return to it repeatedly. In fact, he was one of the very first Jewish intellectuals to break into the teaching of English literature in America.

FRENCH: Trilling's appointment at Columbia, and his subsequent achievement as the first Jew to receive tenure in the English department there, was a milestone in the social progress of the Jewish community. But the possible trauma Irving Howe refers to, with its consequences, was also mentioned by another critic and academic: Alfred Kazin, author of *Walker in the City* and *Starting Out in the Thirties*, two informal volumes of autobiography describing his Jewish boyhood in New York and how he embarked on the literary life. I asked Professor Kazin how he, as a near contemporary from a similar background, viewed Trilling's career.

ALFRED KAZIN: At first I had very mixed feelings. I thought he was extremely able, brilliantly intelligent and very learned, but that he took the whole academic thing much too seriously; it seemed to me also that he was over-conscious of what might be said about him as a New York Jew. One of the most telling incidents in Trilling's life was reported to me by a distinguished classmate of his at Columbia (the class of 1925) whose record was as fine as Trilling's and who in the usual course of events asked for a job there: whereupon the English department, which at that time was, you might say, as Anglican as the House of Lords in the 1850s, said very coldly: 'We have room for only one Jew. We have chosen Mr Trilling.' I always felt myself that Trilling was too much influenced by that experience and became over-cautious because of it. On the other hand I don't think people attain a philosophy for psychological reasons, but because they believe in it: certainly the growing conservatism and academicism – to call it so – fitted in very well with what happened. I should add that Columbia itself of course changed enormously after the war and in the 1950s was no longer the kind of place where such a remark about Jews could have been made.

FRENCH: Things had indeed changed by the fifties. This was clearly the period of Trilling's greatest fame and influence – the forties, fifties and early sixties. Even back in the 1920s he had been known for his reviews in the New York *Evening Post* and was the subject of a couple of lines of verse in 'The Conning Tower', Franklin P. Adams's humorous column for the *New York World*. (That is where Dorothy Parker's 'Men seldom make passes/At girls who wear glasses' appeared.) In 'The Conning Tower' there'd been a jocular couplet on the comic name of the British poet Basil Bunting, which drew the rejoinder: 'To admit defeat we are not willing,/ We have one called Lionel Trilling'.

By the fifties his name was no matter for mirth. In Wallace Markfield's hilarious novel of New York literary

life *To an Early Grave* one of the characters is experiencing
some difficulty in turning out a book review for a literary
journal and sits over his typewriter thus:

> Then he sat.
> Then he took up his match again and peeled four more
> perfect strips . . .
> And he hissed softly, 'Trilling . . . Leavis . . . Ransom
> . . . Tate . . . Kazin . . . Chase . . .' and saw them, The
> Fathers, as though from a vast amphitheatre, smiling
> at him, and he smiled at them.
> And he typed, with a smoking intensity he typed . . .

I spoke about this particular milieu with Norman Podhoretz, editor of the monthly journal *Commentary* – a post
once held by Trilling's mentor and friend the late Elliot
Cohen, who ran the *Menorah Journal* in the late 1920s.

NORMAN PODHORETZ: Trilling was very much of New
York and a prominent figure on the New York scene.
New York in those days – literary New York – was a
world bounded intellectually, and spiritually, by certain
magazines; principally *Partisan Review* and somewhat later
Commentary, but also by the literary quarterlies which
were not actually of New York either physically or spiritually, such as the *Kenyon Review*, the *Sewanee Review* and
others. This was what Randall Jarrell disparagingly called,
in an article in *Partisan Review* in the late forties, the 'age
of criticism'. One can only look back upon this world with
nostalgia from the perspective of a time like the present;
and I've often wondered even so what was so terrible
about it. Jarrell seemed to think that it was self-evidently
a bad thing to be living in an age of criticism, but in fact
there was at that time an enormous amount of intellectual
excitement, associated with an interest in literature and in
the arts generally, with literature at the centre. Literature
itself, with literary study, became something like the
queen, not of the sciences but of the humanities. It played
the kind of cultural role that philosophy and theology
have played at other periods. I think New York became
the symbol for a form of interest in literature that was
broadening rather than parochializing, involving a pas-

sionate concern with its political, social and cultural implications; and to the extent that this was what New York meant to people in other parts of the country (as it did) and that he himself was attracted by this way of thinking about literature and of pursuing a literary vocation, Trilling did represent New York, not exclusively but in those years perhaps pre-eminently.]

FRENCH: Trilling did have something extra that many of the other literary intellectuals hadn't, or not in the same degree – a position of academic eminence; a point that was made by the poet and critic John Hollander.

JOHN HOLLANDER: Unlike a lot of his friends and intellectual associates in New York, he did go through university, take a PhD, teach in graduate school, and engage in that particular tradition, which has become common for us today. Take some of the principal academics in literature in Britain: one thinks of them as part of an intellectual scene as well. This happened here partly through people like Trilling on the one hand, and on the other hand because of that peculiar alliance of the New York intellectuals with the Southern agrarian novelists, poets and critics who were also in the universities – such as Allen Tate, Robert Penn Warren and John Crowe Ransom.

FRENCH: Hollander himself is now part of that literary-intellectual world which unites the university campuses, the cultural journals and the literary pages of the weekly press and is taken so much for granted today. He has just succeeded the novelist Robert Penn Warren in the Department of English at Yale. Thirty years ago Hollander was an undergraduate at Columbia, one of the thousands who have attended Trilling's undergraduate and graduate classes. His contemporaries included a very different kind of poet – Allen Ginsberg, who said of Trilling on his death: 'He had a sweet heart, a sad solemn sweetness'. Hollander now recalls something of what Trilling meant for him as a teacher.

HOLLANDER: The heart of the matter, I think, for my whole generation was that those of us who were either

just too young to have been in World War II, like myself,
or had been in the services when very young, before
coming to college, saw in Lionel a complete reversal of
the American stereotype of the English professor: instead
of a rather clerical, scholarly sort of person here was somebody implicitly and consistently arguing by his concerns,
and by the unique quality of his seriousness, that being
a professor of literature might amount to one of the few
remaining pursuits worth following. I know this was how
he struck my generation, coming to college as I did in the
later forties: he showed us that the study of English was
a serious matter.

FRENCH: Testimony to Trilling's qualities as a teacher
abounds, and teaching was always – this set him apart
too – his primary commitment and great love. Throughout
his life he took a concerned interest in his students and
their affairs. In class he could be formal and detached, but
far from predictable in his views and conduct. One former
pupil recalled him spending an hour addressing an undergraduate class of two hundred, explaining that he had
racked his brains for days and found no inspiration for a
lecture on Kafka's *The Trial*. Another has written of him
putting Camus's *The Rebel* on the list for a course, then
announcing that he'd got around to reading the book and
found he 'couldn't make head nor tail of it', so was throw-
ing it out!

   Norman Podhoretz was a pupil of Trilling's in the post-
war years. He went straight from Columbia to Cambridge,
where he sat at the feet of F. R. Leavis and enjoyed the
rare distinction of writing for Leavis's *Scrutiny* as a student, a review of Trilling's *The Liberal Imagination*. I asked
him what it was like making this transition.

PODHORETZ: In one sense there was a surprising continuity in working with Leavis after studying with Trilling,
in spite of the differences and, to some extent, the hostility
between them. This hostility, indeed, came rather more
from Leavis's side than from Trilling's: Trilling did not
feel any hostility toward Leavis and was always surprised
to discover that Leavis thought less well of him than might
have been expected. In any case for all their differences

they did have similar ideas about the nature of literature and the relation of a work of literature to the historical social cultural context; but as personalities they were very different indeed. Trilling tended to be more tolerant and relaxed about differences of opinion than Leavis, who was of course extremely dogmatic where critical judgment was concerned. One could fall into permanent disfavour with Leavis for liking the wrong poem or enjoying the wrong novel. Leavis had an intensity which was quite foreign to the Trilling temperament. Leavis tended to imbue literary study with a religious passion. I think 'religious' is the precise word, although he himself would certainly have disavowed it. Trilling tended to be rather more agnostic, if you like, in his approach to literature. He was never entirely sure that literature was all that important and he communicated that sense: in fact he once said explicitly, as I remember (shocking some of us aged nineteen and twenty), that there were times when he felt that he would rather do almost anything than read a book. It would be difficult to imagine this kind of statement coming from Leavis, especially in a class-room.

FRENCH: Trilling responded of course to a wider range of literature than Leavis: in respect of English literature, for instance, he was writing that Dickens was one of the two greatest English novelists at a time when Leavis had good words only for *Hard Times*, and no one has written more perceptively or fairly on the Snow-Leavis controversy. Indeed such has been his response to our culture that some have thought he didn't belong in an American tradition at all.

ALFRED KAZIN: I would not agree with that at all: he was very American. What you may be thinking of, and what many have commented on, was his tremendous fondness for your country. I believe his mother had been born in England, though his parents were essentially Russian Jewish immigrants; he had a great feeling for England therefore and was never so happy as when (a) writing about English authors, and (b) living in England, where he held, of course, distinguished posts at Oxford and elsewhere. This was something of a bone of contention

between us, because although I have a tremendous connection myself with England and with English culture and
English books, (like all non-English professors of English
literature) I felt closer frankly to the labour movement and
the working-class tradition in England than I did to
Oxbridge. I didn't see Lionel very often and when we did
meet we often disagreed about developments in England.
I don't know what he thought of what my English friends
called 'the revolution' of the forties and fifties in England,
but my impression was that he tended to overlook it.

FRENCH: That may well be so, but it can hardly be said
that the two works that laid the foundation of Trilling's
reputation have no bearing on the development of post-
war Britain – though their subjects, Matthew Arnold and
E. M. Forster, were Oxbridge men. His *Matthew Arnold*
appeared in 1939 and was the text of his PhD thesis, a
masterly work on a great moralist whom many feel Trilling
himself resembled. There can have been few more sig-
nificant dissertations this century, and it was unusual for
two reasons: it eschewed the consultation of unpublished
materials and it found an immediate general audience.
His shorter book on Forster, then a writer little known in
America, came out in 1943, and in its introductory chapter
he first used the phrase 'liberal imagination'. The obvious
question about his attraction to these authors was a matter
I broached with Stephen Donadio, Associate Editor of
Partisan Review and currently working on a critical biography of Thoreau.

STEPHEN DONADIO: The most obvious similarity
between Trilling and his subjects here, Matthew Arnold
and E. M. Forster, lies in their joint tendency to connect
literary, cultural questions with political matters and to
see the two realms as in some way continuous. It seems
to me that Trilling's work always addressed itself in one
way or another to those continuities between political and
intellectual life – between immediate political circumstances and larger cultural questions – and for this reason
it makes sense that he should have begun writing by
focussing on those two figures. Indeed his work remains
engaged with those questions throughout his career; the

idea that he moves away from what he himself called 'the bloody crossroads' where literature and politics meet, is a fiction. The analysis, in fact, becomes even more far-reaching as he explores further and deeper into the configurations and patterns of thought that manifest themselves in political action in our own time. I'm not sure that this remains true throughout the careers of Arnold and Forster.

The second distinction I would make relates to the importance of modernism in Trilling's career, to the extent that this is concerned with the problem of authority, the whole notion of authority, that is. I think Trilling remains ultimately a modernist – that is to say a critic who recognizes the kinds of tension existing between the claims of the individual self and the claims of society – but that this recognition on his part produces neither ambivalence on the one hand nor simply a submission to the claims of the larger society on the other.

FRENCH: The initial source of that concern for the arts in their social context stemmed partly from an interest in Karl Marx, which began around the time of the Wall Street crash and continued during the early years of the Depression, an event that Trilling experienced both as an intellectual observer and as the sole financial support of his parents and family. His commitment to the far left was relatively brief. He and his immediate circle, as he later wrote (*Middle of the Journey*, p. xv), 'for a short time in 1932 and even into 1933, had been in a tenuous relation with the Communist Party through some of its fringe activities'. This relation didn't last long: the German Communists' role in the rise of Hitler and the conduct of the American Communist Party saw to that. However, when he came to join Jacques Barzun in running that colloquium at Columbia the following year he was still much under the influence of Marx.

BARZUN: At first I thought that his Marxism would keep us apart, because I had no particular interest in, nor any use for, Marxist theorizing, particularly in criticism and the arts; but his Marxism was always a cultural creed, one might say. He was then perhaps at the same stage as

young Marxists are today, going back and back into the
early works of Karl Marx and finding there something far
more wide open and more generous in spirit than the
later formulations which followed the 1859 *Critique of Political Economy*. As his awareness of the practical embodi-
ments of Marxism grew sharper and more intense he fell
away not from Marx's revelations, so to speak, but from
the machinery, the structure and the system. The latter
seemed to him inapplicable to life except in very limited
and severely controlled ways.

FRENCH: It would be wrong, therefore, to think of Trilling
as a Marxist, as one thinks of Edmund Wilson, say, at
that time. Indeed very soon another, more salient influence was to arise, one that would remain constant to the
end – Sigmund Freud. Trilling's understanding of Freud
led to his being the first layman ever invited to give the
Freud Anniversary Lecture at the New York Psychoanal-
ytical Society. And in 1960 he undertook a one-volume
abridgment of Ernest Jones's massive biography of Freud
in order to bring what he considered a key work to a
larger public. Steven Marcus, the Dickens scholar and
author of *The Other Victorians*, collaborated on that abridgment. I asked him what Freud's writings meant to Trilling.

STEVEN MARCUS: First of all it seems to me that Freud
was one of the few systematic thinkers to whom Trilling
responded positively. One of the reasons, I believe, for
his positive response to this particular system-maker or
builder was that Freud's system was singularly open-
ended, so that it could be changed and would be changed
and revised from book to book. Nor did Trilling feel that
the reductive parts of Freud were the essential parts.
Whenever Freud made some reductive or positivist kind
of statement Trilling would tend either to disregard it or
point to something else. I think he was interested in Freud
because his interest in literature was partly a moral one,
partly a psychological one, and partly a cultural one; also
because Freud himself was a great literary figure with an
interest in literature as well, even though it went against
his grain sometimes.

  One of the things that Trilling would often do when

teaching was to draw attention to the literary qualities of Freud's writing, in particular to Freud's unequalled mastery of exposition and argument. I think, however, that Trilling's essential interest in Freud was as a philosopher and psychologist of culture, and as a psychologist who was also a great moralist in some way – pointing to the price that civilization exacts from us – the deformations, maimings and restrictions that it imposes on us all. It seems to me that this part of Freud corresponded closely to Trilling's own sense of what life was like, what life had done to him and how he responded to life; the notion that there is a great deal of sacrifice and renunciation involved, that civilization and culture are painful processes, not simply pleasurable ones; that it's permissible to ask the question 'Is this all worth it?', to which he always had one answer: 'Yes, it is, *but* . . .' That is to say, yes, it's worth it; the price is almost unendurable, but it has to be paid nevertheless.

FRENCH: What did Freud the man mean to Trilling?

MARCUS: He meant a great deal. I think that Freud's tragic stoicism was very important to Trilling; his capacity to bear great amounts of pain both spiritual and physical without complaining – the classical side of Freud – drew Trilling's deep admiration. Also his intellectual boldness, courage and audacity, his willingness to speak out, his refusal to be put down, his ability to live with unpleasantness of one kind or another, his refusal to deviate from what he saw as the truth no matter how unpleasant that truth might seem to others; these were all qualities in Freud that Trilling not only admired but tried to reproduce in himself.

FRENCH: Steven Marcus was reflecting there upon style and personal deportment, which were matters of importance in Trilling's life. He was a strikingly handsome man with a memorable presence, though in no way forbidding. He once quoted Jowett as saying that Matthew Arnold had less 'personality' than any man he knew, meaning not our current use of the word but that 'there was no impulse in Arnold to make special claims for himself, or call attention to himself, or to ask for any indulgence'. That was true of Trilling too; but his style in speech and writing was distinctive.

HOLLANDER: He tended to speak, even casually, with a very careful manner. It was not that he spoke prose, that sounds terribly artificial. There are few people who speak prose (Monsieur Jourdain was wrong – we do not speak prose, we speak speech). Trilling always spoke in well-formed sentences and he was extremely witty. His literary style was characterized both by a kind of controlled passion and by a great elegance that was not in despite of that controlled passion. The prose of his novel, *The Middle of the Journey*, has a kind of willed and systematic greyness, it seems to me. I believe this was his intention and that he was very conscious at the time of writing of wanting to produce a novel of ideas; and that he saw the need of turning away from that tradition in the American novel which always brings it close to romance. One is therefore highly conscious of his style at all times.

FRENCH: John Hollander brings up there the matter of Trilling's fiction which, setting aside those early uncollected tales, amounts to the novel *The Middle of the Journey* and two superb and frequently anthologized short stories: 'Of this time, of that place', a haunting study of a college teacher's confrontation with a mad pupil, and 'The other Margaret' (all written within the space of a few years in the mid-forties). Why he didn't write any more fiction is something of a puzzle, as these works rank among the best of their day and stand up to frequent re-reading. I have been told it is because he received no encouragement from American publishers and editors to write more, which is sad indeed. One could infer this from the lack of any attempt to sell *The Middle of the Journey* to its enthusiastic British publisher, Frederic Warburg. In Warburg's memoirs we read that the head of the New York publishing house from whom Warburg bought it hadn't bothered to read the book a week before it came out! Though it was begun apparently as a novella about a coming to terms with death (a recurrent and entirely unmorbid theme in Trilling's writings), *The Middle of the Journey* became a

political novel, worthy to be compared with Forster's fiction or Henry James's *Princess Casamassima*. I discussed
the ways in which it differed from the political fiction of
its time with Professor Daniel Aaron of Harvard, a literary
historian and author of a key study of the 1930s, *Writers
on the Left*; and he invoked first of all Trilling's short story
'The other Margaret', a tale of a middle-class New York
girl being awakened to certain realities of existence.

DANIEL AARON: Interestingly enough the figures that
are chosen to represent the working-class – the maid, and
the bus conductor who frightens the little girl – are sym-
bols of that darker reality which the liberal imagination
refuses to accept. This is rather paradoxical and decidedly
anti-thirties, because in the thirties, you remember, it was
the proletarian who was good and wholesome and noble,
while the bourgeois figures were wicked and mean and
sly and cowardly. Thus Trilling almost seems to be revers-
ing the positions. I think this disturbed some readers,
who must have wondered why the figures representing
what was evil should be working-class or near working-
class, such as the hired man in *The Middle of the Journey*:
it's about as far away from the usual kind of proletarian
saga of the 1930s as you can imagine. There were very
few novels of that time, among those I can recall, which
adopted this attitude. Because of the celebration of the
working-class the story usually hinged on the gradual
awareness of the middle-class hero or heroine that society
was closing in on them so that they had to choose between
the defunct capitalist class and the rising working class.
Trilling's *The Middle of the Journey* is a reversal of those
pieties and a corrective, some would say to excess; there's
a certain bitterness, a certain coldness, a certain snobbish-
ness, some might even say, in the values that are explicitly
stated or implied in this novel.

FRENCH: After a quiet reception in 1947 the book became
briefly the centre of controversy some years later through
the identification of its central character Gifford Maxim
with the ex-communist Whittaker Chambers, a Columbia
contemporary of Trilling's, though never a close friend,
and the accuser of Alger Hiss. To be more exact, it brought

Lionel Trilling into this controversy, for the novel itself
was rather left behind.

The author's own account of this affair is to be found
in the introduction to the new British edition of the novel
that appeared shortly before his death. Quentin Anderson
deals with the way in which *The Middle of the Journey*
relates to the central issues of Trilling's writings, to such
key preoccupations as 'the self' and 'the will'.

ANDERSON: In this novel a figure who in some ways
resembles Trilling himself deals with a political crisis in
his own life, or rather a crisis which is both personal and
political in his own life and in that of friends whom he
visits in Connecticut; and what the book moves toward is
an apprehension that among these friends politics is serv-
ing an immediate personal need and is thereby removed
from its ostensible goal – the amelioration of human
affairs. This perception, which I think is a sturdy one
about American intellectual life, still thrums for me in that
book as one of the most vivid accounts you could possibly
find of how it is that American intellectuals have become
related to politics. One might elaborate on it a little and
say that the taste for apocalypse among American intellectuals has often served to obscure their sense of political
actuality in a way which it is indeed hard for me to convey
to my English friends. It might also be said that one can
scarcely blame Americans for this kind of extravagant
devotion to an idea which serves their sense of themselves, because clearly it's harder for us to strike out a
sense of our own personal being from the iron of American circumstances; yet the fact remains that this still affects
the nature of American intellectual life, that when we turn
to what we call politics it frequently seems to be rather a
way of expanding our sense of ourselves than of encoun-
tering some immediate social reality.

You speak of the will: 'the will' became toward the end
of Trilling's life a preoccupation, the term that he himself
chose to employ to suggest that a resignation of will in
joining a cause might well be a resignation of one's intellectual and moral convictions as well; that unless people
gathered about a question, so to speak, with their full

selfhood present, the discussion was not a real discussion but simply an exchange of sufficient attitudes; is mine more sufficient than yours? If so perhaps you should join in mine, although in so doing you would destroy your own independence. This was a continuing preoccupation for him. It led toward the end of his life to the feeling on the part of many people that he was not taking part in politics. I believe it would be more accurate to say that he had found that most of what people called political preoccupations were not in fact political but simply a way of assuring themselves that they had a proper fullness of being: hence his emphasis on the term 'will'. He was thinking in a rather old-fashioned sense, perhaps, of nineteenth-century assertions of will, of the sort of discovery of the nature of political process that a nineteenth-century prophet undertook to make and then to pronounce upon (I use the term 'prophet' in the Carlyle/Ruskin/Arnold/Mill tradition). This led to a view that Trilling was conservative or reactionary, whereas it seems to me that in fact he was seeking the substance of politics.

FRENCH: After the publication of *The Middle of the Journey*, explicitly political reflections – except where they figure retrospectively in memoirs – are infrequently encountered in Trilling's writings. I asked Jacques Barzun if this was an aberrant, insensitive British reading of his work.

BARZUN: No, I think it is quite true that although the political implications were always there the political statements became fewer. Furthermore I would venture the thought that the novel was a kind of turning-point in that respect – that he purged all his political feeling of a polemical sort in that work.

FRENCH: This leads us on to some peculiarly tricky ground. Explicitly polemical and political writing is not something one associates with Lionel Trilling. One does associate it, however, with his wife Diana, the literary critic and social observer, whom he married in 1929. As any reader of her articles or her two books *Claremont Essays* and *We Must March My Darlings* will know, she is a formidable debater with positively forensic gifts. Yet the heart of Trilling's writings is political, as Quentin Anderson says, and as Norman Podhoretz made clear when I asked him what it was that made Trilling a controversial figure.

PODHORETZ: I believe that he was mainly controversial for political reasons, and that this has been obfuscated by much of what has been written about him since his death. There has been an unseemly and over-hasty effort to assimilate him to the ages; and although there will be time for that it does seem to me that Trilling was so anchored and so rooted in the political cultural polemics of his day, I find that it falsifies Trilling to talk about him in the large and rather abstract terms in which he has been talked about in many of the obituary pieces. My belief is that it is impossible to understand either what he was saying throughout his literary career, or the response to what he was saying, without talking bluntly about the issue of communism, or Stalinism if you like, together with the role that communism, Stalinism, played in American culture from the early 1930s right up to this very moment. Trilling was a central figure in the de-mystification of the Stalinist mentality, particularly as it affected cultural issues; and if you miss that element in his writing I think you miss what is central to his writing. It seems to me that in his last years he himself was reluctant to be as plain, as clear, as blunt on this issue as he had been in an earlier period. This may have damaged him as a writer, but I don't believe it changed the essential thrust of what he was getting at in almost everything he wrote.

FRENCH: The central document here would be *The Liberal Imagination* of 1950, subtitled 'Essays on Literature and Society': sixteen articles and lectures on fiction, Freud, the Kinsey Report, and so on. In an extract from an unpublished lecture of 1974 that his widow and son James, (an art historian), decided to include as a foreword to a new edition of the book, Trilling himself invokes the word 'Stalinism' as the rigid and corrupt form of thinking from which he was recalling the liberal intellect to its duty. In this particular context the term 'liberal' is not immediately intelligible to British readers, and I asked Irving Howe, who styles himself a socialist, to comment on it.

IRVING HOWE: The word 'socialism' in this country still has a somewhat disreputable flavour and so people tend to use 'liberalism' as a cover-all term which, it is understood, sometimes includes leftism or socialism. As Trilling used the word, however, it would also include a kind of conservatism, since his basic political point of view might be described as a conservative version of liberalism: that is, in regard to issues on which militancy, for example, was important in this country, he tended to be conservative. His sense of liberalism was that of an open society, tolerance, humaneness, generosity; it was more a moral imaginative stance than a concrete politics, and in that respect I think he was entirely admirable. His sense of liberalism at times was almost the equivalent of moral imagination, of richness, diversity, complexity, openness of mind.

FRENCH: Morris Dickstein, who spoke at the beginning of this discussion about the crucial role *The Liberal Imagination* played in his intellectual development in the 1950s, has been giving considerable thought to Trilling's influence in the course of writing his cultural history of the sixties, *Gates of Eden*. He continues Irving Howe's analysis.

DICKSTEIN: One of the principal ambiguities in *The Liberal Imagination* is what sort of liberalism precisely Trilling is referring to. One way of reading it is to see the book as an attempt to bring up to date, and perhaps to close off once and for all, a debate that really dealt with Stalinism rather than liberalism. Stalinism had been the great issue that had agitated Trilling and his circle in the thirties and to some extent in the forties; and in some ways liberalism is a code word in that book not simply for Stalinism but for all attempts to politicize literature in a gross and vulgar way, to engage it directly toward political action or to look at writers from what is mainly or even covertly a political perspective. I think that's why in the opening chapter Trilling deals with Parrington: he's particularly angry at Parrington's preference for a writer like Dreiser over a

he disliked restrictions
placed on literature by
Stalinism

writer like Henry James, and he clearly feels that it's Parrington's progressive politics that prevent him from recog-
nizing the virtues of a more conservative figure like James,
as opposed to an overtly left-wing writer like Dreiser. An
interesting parallel here is the Hungarian Marxist George
Lukács, one of whose famous pieces of analysis of the
realistic novel reveals his preference for the conservative
Balzac over the overtly radical Zola; in this Lukács follows
Marx and Engels, although Zola's politics, the overt politics in his life at least, are closer, clearly, to those of Marx
or Lukács himself. Lukács believed that the conservative
Balzac – in Trilling's case the conservative Henry James
– had a deeper sense of class and of the structure of
society than the more radical figure, who tended to flatten
things out from an ideological perspective. Thus you
might say that *The Liberal Imagination*, which is, in my
opinion, Trilling's most important book of criticism, is
trying to free the imagination from the constraints not
 simply of liberalism, but from any political perspective
whatsoever; and to do that is in itself a political judgment,
a political act. It is a way of reaching a broader kind of
politics based upon the amplitude of a work of the imagination, directed not only toward criticism but toward one's
political goals and the possibility of political action. R. P.
Blackmur, the author of one of the early pieces on Trilling
in the fifties, objected that there could be no such thing
as real politics with the amplitude and ambiguity of vision
of any work of literature, maintaining further that to apply
such a standard inevitably led either to a conservative
position or to a withdrawal from politics, because no political activity could ever be as fine as the kind of literary
judgment or the degree of consciousness to be found in
a Henry James novel; and I think this was a shrewd judgment on Blackmur's part. It was written at a time when
Trilling did seem to be a very political figure, yet it clearly
anticipated his considerable withdrawal from politics after
The Liberal Imagination, whereby he lost, to my mind, some
of its ambivalence. It was somehow both a literary and a
political work, whereas Trilling's later work is often much
more directly literary. The attempt to develop a finer sort
of politics, using works of the imagination as models,

would seem to have failed for him in his own estimation; thereupon he pulled back to the imagination alone, and many of us who had responded precisely to that connection of literature and politics did not feel as moved or as deeply involved with some of Trilling's very fine later work as with *The Liberal Imagination*.

FRENCH: Alfred Kazin too notes an ambiguity in Trilling's writings and stance of that time, but interprets it in a different way.

KAZIN: A great deal of Trilling's influence came from the fact that he spoke for a generation that didn't want to resolve its contradictions – unwilling to become openly anti-liberal on the one hand but on the other hand eager to shake off with revulsion whatever connection it had had earlier with Marxism and all it stood for. This attitude itself had a lot to do with the fact that the United States became very prosperous in the forties and fifties, and in the early sixties. Another important factor was that a great many people at Columbia and elsewhere, students of Trilling's, had been tremendous disciples of his. Many well-known writers and editors throughout the country owed a great deal to him; others became more radicalized and felt irritated by what they saw as a certain addiction to the *status quo*, so to speak; and America is not a very easy country in which to be addicted in such a way, since life changes all the time so rapidly and so violently that it seems incongruous to think of people adopting a conservative position. As Trilling himself lamented in one of his essays, there is no American conservatism properly speaking, only liberals in various stages of change, I would say. In fact this tradition of liberalism, radicalism, whatever you like to call it, was a position which Trilling was never happy with but could never be totally *un*happy with; and this argument with himself, as he put it, was exactly what gave so many academics, especially in the fifties, a feeling of satisfaction. It led to a certain sense of intellectual nicety and intellectual elegance, which fitted in very well with things until the sixties came, when it turned out that the young were not interested in criticism any more, nor were they much interested in literature at all, but wrote and

spoke like barbarians; which might be satisfying to the
old curmudgeons but seemed to point to something very
wrong in American education, since these were our own
students.

FRENCH: Professor Kazin has mentioned the campus
revolts of the 1960s, by which Trilling was inevitably
affected, both as a thinker and as a teacher. Naturally he
was most directly affected by the disruptions at Columbia
in 1968, and by the accompanying obscenities and viol-
ence. Stephen Donadio recalled that Trilling was especially depressed by what he regarded as the gratuitous
political activity of the majority – the serious radicals he
could at least understand. I asked Dr Donadio what permanent effects the experience had on Trilling's thinking.

DONADIO: It seems to me that the sense of polarization,
and the particular identification between the university
and society at large that prevailed at Columbia in 1968,
were factors Trilling regarded as threatening the future of
universities in general and intellectual discourse as well;
and I don't think he was wholly convinced at the time of
his death that this sort of facile identification had ceased.
I believe he retained the sense that a blow had been struck
not simply against any particular institution, but against
the concept of mind and the functioning of mind in modern life. This danger might or might not be overcome in
the future but he was not entirely convinced that it was
a passing phase.

FRENCH: The latter sections of *Sincerity and Authenticity*
and Trilling's 1972 Thomas Jefferson Award Lecture on
'Mind in the Modern World' reflect his concern for the
assaults upon reason and civility launched by the disturb-
ances of the sixties. Did they also affect his allegiance to
the modern in literature and his attitude to the apocalyptic
impulse the modernists tended to embody in the so-called
'adversary project' – the notion that the aware individual
was in opposition to his society? 'The self in its standing
quarrel with culture' is a phrase that recurs in slightly
varying forms throughout his work. Trilling had belonged
to a generation which had identified with the modern in

culture and the radical (though anti-communist) in politics
– an association forged by, and ultimately turned into
something of an orthodoxy by, the group of intellectuals
surrounding the reformed *Partisan Review* of the late thirties (Trilling served on the magazine's advisory board for
many years). *Partisan Review* could publish left-wing
polemics, yet still be thought a fit place by T. S. Eliot for
his *East Coker* to make its first American appearance. For
a time, George Orwell, a writer admired by Trilling, contributed a regular 'Letter from London'. Morris Dickstein
spoke to me of what he considers Trilling's changing attitude to 'the moderns'.

DICKSTEIN: When Trilling came of age in the thirties
American culture was still to a great extent under the
domination of middle-brow organs of literature and literary criticism – the remnants of the New England genteel
tradition in American letters. He even contributed two
essays to a book edited by Malcolm Cowley, called *Beyond
the Genteel Tradition* as I remember. For the writers of
Trilling's generation, figures like Kafka and Proust and
Joyce almost seemed like weapons to be used against this
decaying brahmin tradition in America; and I think his
commitment to modernism was probably a good deal
stronger then, in the thirties and forties. With the disin-
tegration of the tradition he was opposing (much like the
tradition of Sunday journalism in England opposed by
Leavis in his early days), modern culture – American culture at least – moved violently, perhaps excessively, in
the direction Trilling had long been favouring; and he felt,
especially in the sixties, that the entire culture became
modernist. In my book I quote Trilling as saying that the
student movements of the sixties with their subversive
character, their salvational aims, their utopianism, their
desire for extreme and intense experience, could be
described as 'modernism in the streets'. I don't think he
meant that it was modernism *per se*, or those writers
belonging to the movement, which had directly influenced the younger generation of the sixties. What happened was, I believe, that Trilling's ambivalence
developed in seeing what modernism really meant when

applied to life itself, when it was taken out of a library and brought into the street and became a political movement. After all, writers like Yeats and Eliot, though their politics were very seamy and proto-fascist in some ways, never really became involved in actual political activity; whereas something quite different happened in the sixties. I think that Trilling now began to withdraw to another kind of literature for which he has always had a great affinity – the great tradition of nineteenth-century realism – and that both his literary tastes and his political affinities shifted toward a much more conservative standpoint, akin to that of Stendhal, Balzac, Dickens and George Eliot as opposed to the more extreme experience represented by Kafka, Proust and so on.

FRENCH: It is possible to see Trilling's developing attitude to modernism in a slightly different way.

DONADIO: One of the things that Trilling resisted was the facile acceptance of apocalyptic notions, as if they meant nothing at all and had no social consequences – the worship of the void or the abyss or whatever, as if that were simply a literary idea. It seems to me that his insistence was always that literary ideas are not merely ideas: that they do have social consequences, the great difficulty being to recognize a certain threat embodied in the very nature of modern experience and somehow to overcome it. What he objected to therefore, as I see it, was the idea of domesticating these ideas so that they simply became fashionable and without content. It was this aspect of modernism with which he had no patience, for he took modernism so seriously that he recognized its power, fully realizing that this could be used to do considerable damage as well as to effect progress.

FRENCH: In the light of what Stephen Donadio says, it is not surprising that Lionel Trilling should attach such importance to Joseph Conrad's story *Heart of Darkness* – regarding it as in some sense paradigmatic. Two other early adherents of modernism – slightly older contemporaries of Trilling's – were also to turn away from its more advanced stages, though somewhat querulously and without Trilling's grace. I refer to Edmund Wilson and F. R. Leavis. They're critics who belong together, not merely because of their eminence – I asked Stephen Marcus if he agreed that it made sense to link Trilling with them.

MARCUS: Associating Trilling with Leavis and Wilson is to put him in the right place, because they do go together. There is a commonalty of discourse among them, it seems to me. None of these distinguished critics had a particular method that could be circumscribed, defined and applied by anyone else. All of them remained resolutely within a general realm of critical discourse; that is to say, a realm of discourse which, however formal in its cadences, nevertheless refused to fall into a specific critical language or to use a specific critical method so that it could be taught in courses, in schools, as it were. In fact the discourse they all maintained was a general discourse – clearly an inheritance of the great nineteenth-century critical discourse, in all three instances, carrying on from John Stuart Mill, Matthew Arnold and the other great nineteenth-century critics. What this means is that all three – though I'm speaking particularly of Trilling here – could write about literature and yet not invoke a special language for it, could use literature to evoke more general topics of broad interest and could, in fine, speak about the bearing of literature upon cultural, moral and personal issues of importance in human affairs, just as the great nineteenth-century critics and prose writers did. This seems to me to be one of the distinctive qualities about Trilling as a critic.

FRENCH: Earlier on Norman Podhoretz spoke of the relations between Trilling and Leavis. Those between Trilling and Wilson were warmer and more interesting. As literary editor of *New Republic* in the late twenties, Wilson gave the young Trilling his first books to review for a major journal. When Wilson's novel *Memoirs of Hecate County* was prosecuted for obscenity in the mid-forties, Trilling appeared as a defence witness. Their relationship was one of the things I discussed with Daniel Aaron, a friend of Wilson's and editor of his correspondence.

AARON: It's very interesting to me to compare the two

men, because they were often regarded by their rival partisans as somehow in competition with one another. They knew each other from the early thirties on, and I believe they always maintained very friendly relations. Wilson had been very encouraging to Trilling when the latter was working on Matthew Arnold. This was at a time when many of his New York associates who had become committed to the Left felt that, in writing about Arnold, Trilling was turning his back on the real issues of his time, to some extent. Wilson was at that time much involved in politics, in his Marxist phase – always sceptically Marxist but deeply interested in social matters and writing about them, and also concerned primarily then, as later, with literature. Anybody who was doing serious work in literature belonged to his company. There's an amusing incident in one of Trilling's fugitive pieces where he describes a situation when he was working on Arnold and feeling rather low, nobody talking to him. Going into a men's room he met Wilson there: Wilson immediately asked him what he was working on and discovering that Arnold was his subject told him how interested he was, and to be sure and let him know when the book was finished. This gave Trilling an enormous lift. He was concerned, however, as to whether he was doing the right thing by teaching, and this may have created some difference between them. Nothing open, nothing sharp, but a sense perhaps that he, Trilling, had committed himself to the academic life while Wilson had remained the free-wheeling journalist, cutting himself off deliberately from the academic world which he felt was somehow debilitating for the creative imagination.

FRENCH: Some feel that it was the exigencies of the academic life with its heavy teaching programme that restricted Trilling's literary output, making his *oeuvre* a good deal smaller than Wilson's: two biographies, a novel and a series of lectures represent Lionel Trilling's only book-length works. However the collections of essays are not thrown together, but selected for their relation to a particular theme; and the essays themselves were not knocked off. They are examples of what Norman Podhoretz extolled in an essay of his from the 1950s called 'The Article as Art', a view to which Podhoretz still holds.

PODHORETZ: The milieu out of which he came, the New York literary intellectual world of his day, specialized, you might say, in the essay or the article or even the book review as a literary genre: New York intellectuals wrote essays and reviews with the kind of seriousness and intensity and commitment that one associates with the writing of poetry rather than with the writing of journalism. It's impossible to imagine anyone writing anything with a greater intensity and seriousness of purpose than people in that milieu brought to their articles and reviews; and if one is willing to accept that such writing is an art form, as I was and continue to be, then certainly Trilling stood out as one of its pre-eminent practitioners, one of the most elegant, perhaps *the* most elegant of the essayists of that style.

FRENCH: Yet for all that pre-eminence – a poll conducted in 1970 among the US intelligentsia placed him as one of the top ten most prestigious contemporary American intellectuals – there are those who think Trilling hasn't had his full due, or rather that in the latter years of his life his standing was not as high as it should have been. One of these is Jacques Barzun.

BARZUN: In this country it's rather difficult to obtain the kind of recognition which Trilling deserved, in my opinion, unless one takes a very sharply marked attitude, a stance for some gimmick or point of view or slogan. The very essence of the critical method for Lionel Trilling, however, was that there was no such method; that one used the entire resources of the human mind upon the multitude of issues presented or implied by a piece of work and then gave the result literary form. Moreover, in view of the increasing rapidity with which schools succeed each other, formulas becoming clichés and clichés a bore, I fear it's going to be less and less possible for thoughtful work to receive attention, let alone recognition. Then again Trilling's life and ways, his perfect civility and calm, even serenity, did not lend themselves to news stories

enigmatic

which would have fixed his mind in the public eye. He didn't knock anyone down off a stool in a bar. He led a very respectable and modest existence. Socially he was not domineering or egotistical or eccentric in any way. In other words he lacked all the features that are needed to publicize in our rather raucous age.

FRENCH: That may be so: indeed many of the traits Barzun notes in Trilling are those Trilling himself noted in the superficially unexciting life of Matthew Arnold. There has been a Trilling Seminar established at Columbia, however, to engage regularly with themes that interested him; a collection of essays in his honour with the appropriate title *Art, Politics, and Will* has recently appeared; and there are numerous books about him in various stages of completion – anything between seven and a dozen. Estimates of their number vary. Edmund Wilson with a lifetime of colourful behaviour and numerous sexual escapades has yet to be the subject of one sizeable study since his death. Steven Marcus sees several reasons for this.

MARCUS: First of all, there is clearly something enigmatic about Trilling, part of the enigma being where did this mind come from, how did it create itself and why did it take the turns that it did, turns which were often unpredictable. Secondly, there is an enigma about what this mind was really up to, what were its fundamental assumptions, because the writing is very subtle and complex and doesn't often say overtly what its assumptions are. Thirdly, we are coming to the end of a political era and the beginning of a new era, as we always are, and the political component in Trilling's work – in his writings about literature and culture, that is – has vexed people considerably. Some people have been for it, others against it. Probably more have been against it than for it in recent years; and as the era of political unrest recedes, it's quite natural that a figure like Trilling who was commenting upon a good deal of this indirectly and in his own way, should be re-examined.

FRENCH: Among those who, it seems to me, have been arduously wrestling with Trilling's writings over the years is Irving Howe, a founding editor in the 1950s of the influential left-wing journal *Dissent*.

HOWE: Your description is right. There has been a certain process of wrestling on my part. We became friendly when I was a very young man, and he was extremely helpful and generous to me. He was a deeply generous man. Our friendship began in the early years of my career as a writer, which would have been in the late 1940s; then there was a kind of intellectual falling out in the fifties and a reconciliation some years later, and toward the last seven or eight years of his life we were quite good friends. This was not a personal matter mainly or exclusively, however. I recognized that in the fifties there really was a genuine political intellectual divergence, and it was very hard to put up with that. It was difficult to understand ths nature of it, for I continued to admire his criticism intensely even during those years, as he knew, though we didn't see very much of each other at that time. Later, during the late sixties, when we both felt somewhat under siege and were being attacked by the New Left, the differences between us were submerged in the general, rhetorical barrage from that quarter. We tacitly recognized, I think, that our political intellectual divergence remained but that we shared a great many literary and cultural values. I would like to think that in the process I myself developed and grew, and came to understand the extraordinary gifts he possessed, indeed more than extraordinary gifts, in the plural; that he was a writer who gave *us* a gift, the gift he gave us being the sense that even in a bad time, such as the years in which we have lived, the imagination – the capacity to see and enlarge and create – still had a life and autonomy of its own; that we weren't simply bound down by circumstances, or to use his phrase 'conditioned'.

FRENCH: John Hollander took a similar view of the enduring legacy of Trilling's work.

HOLLANDER: I think this may be defined as a kind of moral seriousness and a firm belief in the nobility and power of one of the meanings of the word 'culture'. This was what he always stood for, faithfully representing it without a trace of naivety about the ravages that history could work on one's ability to use one's mind, powerfully and gracefully.

FRENCH: There was nothing bludgeoning about his methods and no easy soliciting of opinions or engineering of consent. Stephen Donadio makes a crucial point about Trilling's approach.

DONADIO: He was not inclined to knock down straw men: if he challenged a position he always did so at its strongest point, attacking what might be regarded as its fullest, most complete and intellectually defensible aspect: the point of its greatest authority, if you will. He challenged that exact point, not some ludicrous version of it. For that reason his judgments had a power which to my mind is lacking in the case of many critics who aim at easy targets and make facile judgments carrying no weight. The whole question of liberalism is very much to the point here. To take *The Liberal Imagination* or *The Middle of the Journey*, I think one has the sense there that what he is objecting to in politically liberal tendencies consists of everything that is programmatic, mechanical, narrow and mindless finally; and that both of those works have the variety and the complexity he asks for in the liberal imagination.

FRENCH: And which of these writings will especially endure?

BARZUN: I believe the essays as a whole (in which I would include the Matthew Arnold and the E. M. Forster) will endure, both for their positive declarative statements about their subject matter as well as for all the implications of these presentations and for the asides that occur in every paragraph. This means to me that Lionel Trilling is one of the great critics. He's a Coleridge, he's a Matthew Arnold, he's a Walter Bagehot; he is less monumental than Hazlitt but he belongs to that tradition of great critics who make of criticism not a work of art (I don't think he would have professed to do that, nor do I believe that criticism can ever be a work of art in the same sense as a novel, a poem or a play), yet who raise criticism to the category of a philosophy, social, political and metaphysical.

FRENCH: Finally, in the absence of a theory to be taken and applied, I asked Quentin Anderson what it is that Lionel Trilling has left us, what will we *use* from him?

ANDERSON: We would first of all, I hope, use his most strongly enforced negative, which is that to be a critic in the world not simply of books but of human actuality one can't have a sufficient method, for there is no such thing. The positive involved here is, I think, that Trilling's adjuration to us remains: can you accept your full humanity and that of others; can you accept the fact that we can't put all our eggs in the basket of art, that we can't confine all our moral convictions to some systematic programme; that we must bear the full responsibility of our lives, whether we talk about art, about politics or about morality; that this is indeed a heavy responsibility but that I speak to you and ask an answer in judgment. This sounds almost Kantian and perhaps too dry; but one should make one's judgments fully personal. One should never isolate art from politics, nor from the human will and the human intention.

Bibliography

EDMUND WILSON

I Thought of Daisy (1929). This novel was not published in Britain until 1952 and in 1957 was reissued in America with the early story *Galahad*.

Axel's Castle: a study in the imaginative literature of 1870–1930 (1930).

The Triple Thinkers: ten essays on literature (1938, enlarged to twelve essays in 1948).

To the Finland Station: a study in the writing and acting of history (1940, revised 1973).

The Wound and the Bow: seven studies in literature (1941).

Memoirs of Hecate County (1946). These linked fictions were reissued in a revised and unexpurgated edition in 1958.

Europe Without Baedeker: sketches among the ruins of Italy, Greece and England (1947; republished in 1967 with *Notes from a European Diary 1963–1964*).

Classics and Commercials: a literary chronicle of the forties (1950).

The Shores of Light: a literary chronicle of the twenties and thirties (1952).

Five Plays: Cyprian's Prayer, The Crime in the Whistler Room, This Room and This Gin and These Sandwiches, Beppo and Beth, The Little Blue Light (1954).

The Scrolls from the Dead Sea (1955); greatly extended in 1969 as *The Dead Sea Scrolls 1947–1969*.

Red Black Blond and Olive: studies in four civilizations: Zuni, Haiti, Soviet Russia, Israel (1956).

A Piece of My Mind: reflections at sixty (1957).

The American Earthquake: a documentary of the twenties and thirties (1958).

Apologies to the Iroquois (1960).

Night Thoughts, his selected poems (1961).

Patriotic Gore: studies in the literature of the Civil War (1962).

The Cold War and the Income Tax: a protest (1963).

The Bit Between My Teeth: a literary chronicle of 1950–1965 (1965).

O Canada: an American's notes on Canadian culture (1965).

A Prelude: landscapes, characters and conversations from the earlier years of my life (1967).

The Duke of Palermo and Other Plays, with an Open Letter to Mike Nichols (1969).

Upstate: records and recollections of Northern New York (1971).

A Window on Russia for the use of Foreign Readers (1972).

The Devils and Canon Barham: ten essays on poets, novelists and monsters (1973).

The Twenties: from notebooks and diaries of the period, edited by Leon Edel (1975).

Letters on Literature and Politics 1912–1972, edited by Elena Wilson (1977).

The Nabokov–Wilson Letters: correspondence between Vladimir Nabokov and Edmund Wilson 1940–1971, edited by Simon Karlinsky (1979).

As editor, Wilson's two most important works are *The Shock of Recognition: the development of literature in the United States recorded by the men who made it* (1943), and *The Crack-Up, with other uncollected pieces, notebooks and unpublished letters* by F. Scott Fitzgerald (1945).

ON EDMUND WILSON

Sherman Paul: *Edmund Wilson: a study of the literary vocation in our time* (1965).

Charles P. Frank: *Edmund Wilson* (1970).

Leonard Kriegel: *Edmund Wilson* (1970).

Richard David Ramsey: *Edmund Wilson: a bibliography* (1971).

Clive James: 'Edmund Wilson and the end of the American Dream' (*Times Literary Supplement*, 19 May 1972, unsigned). Reprinted in James's *The Metropolitan Critic* (1974).

The Times, 13 June 1972, obituary: 'Mr Edmund Wilson, a brilliant American writer and critic'.

Frederick Exley: *Pages from Cold Island*, a remarkable volume of autobiography (sequel to *A Fan's Notes*) by an

American writer and teacher, starting as a meditation on the death of Edmund Wilson (1975).

John Wain (editor): *An Edmund Wilson Celebration*, a symposium containing essays on Wilson by David Flusser, Andrew Harvey, Clive James, Alfred Kazin, Bette Crouse Mele, Helen Muchnic, Edith Olivier, Peter Sharratt, John Updike, John Wain, Angus Wilson and Larzer Ziff (1978).

F. R. LEAVIS

New Bearings in English Poetry: a study of the contemporary situation (1932).

Culture and Environment: the training of critical awareness with Denys Thompson (1933).

Revaluation: tradition and development in English poetry (1936).

The Great Tradition: George Eliot, Henry James, Joseph Conrad (1948).

The Common Pursuit (1952).

D. H. Lawrence, Novelist (1956).

Anna Karenina and Other Essays (1967).

English Literature in Our Time and the University (1969).

Lectures in America – with Q. D. Leavis (1969).

Dickens the Novelist – with Q. D. Leavis (1970)

Nor Shall My Sword: discourses on pluralism, compassion and social hope (1972).

Letters in Criticism (1974).

The Living Principle: 'English' as a discipline of thought (1975).

Thoughts, Words and Creativity: art and thought in Lawrence (1976).

Scrutiny was reprinted in 1963 in twenty volumes with an index and a retrospective essay by Dr Leavis. In 1968 he edited *A Selection from Scrutiny* in two volumes. Earlier, in 1948, Eric Bentley edited his own selection called *The Importance of Scrutiny*.

ON F. R. LEAVIS

Ronald Hayman: *Leavis* (1976).
The Times, 18 April 1978: obituary

New Statesman, 21 April 1978: 'Symposium F. R. Leavis
    1895–1978', with contributions from George Steiner,
    Geoffrey Grigson, Kingsley Amis, David Lodge, D. J.
    Enright, Ian Hamilton, John Bayley, Clive James and
    Malcolm Bradbury.
Francis Mulhern: *The Moment of 'Scrutiny'* (1979). This
    Marxist study in the sociology of literature and culture
    contains an extensive bibliography.
John Harvey: 'F. R. Leavis: an appreciation' (*Encounter*,
    May 1979).
William Walsh: *F. R. Leavis* (1980).

LIONEL TRILLING

Matthew Arnold (1939).
E. M. Forster: a study (1943; revised edition 1967).
The Middle of the Journey (1947). This novel was reissued
    with a new introduction in 1975.
The Liberal Imagination: essays on literature and society (1950).
The Opposing Self: nine essays in criticism (1956).
A Gathering of Fugitives (1956).
Beyond Culture: essays on literature and learning (1965).
Mind in the Modern World (1973).

A Uniform Edition of Trilling's work is being published
by Harcourt Brace Jovanovich, and so far *Matthew Arnold*,
The Opposing Self, *Beyond Culture*, *A Gathering of Fugitives*,
The Liberal Imagination, and *Of This Time, Of That Place and
Other Stories* have appeared. This edition will contain three
volumes of uncollected and unpublished articles that will
include a long essay 'The Changing Myth of the Jew',
written for the *Menorah Journal* in 1931, set in type but not
published until three years after his death (*Commentary*,
August 1978).
    Of Trilling's various anthologies *The Portable Matthew
Arnold* (1949) remains in print and is essential, while *The
Experience of Literature: a reader with commentaries* (1967) is
a marvellous compilation but long out of print. The introduction to Robert Warshow's collected criticism *The
Immediate Experience* (1962), and the afterword to a paper-

back reissue of Tess Slesinger's 1934 novel *The Unpossessed* (1966) are particularly revealing personal essays.

ABOUT LIONEL TRILLING

Nathan Scott: *Three American Moralists: Mailer, Bellow, Trilling* (1973).

The Times, 10 November 1975, obituary: 'Professor Lionel Trilling, a literary critic of major stature'.

Philip Lopate: 'Remembering Lionel Trilling' in *American Review*, 25 (1976).

Robert Boyers: *Lionel Trilling* (1973).

John Bayley: 'The Way Towards Sanity' (*Times Literary Supplement*, 30 December 1977), a review of Robert Boyers's monograph.

Quinton Anderson, Stephen Donadio, Steven Marcus (Editors): *Art, Politics and Will: essays in honour of Lionel Trilling* (1977): Contains essays by Jacques Barzun, Gertrude Himmelfarb, Edward W. Said, Fritz Stern, Frank Kermode, Robert M. Adams, Richard Hoggart, Daniel Bell, and the three editors.

Diana Trilling: 'Lionel Trilling, a Jew at Columbia' (*Commentary*, March 1979), an essay that will be the foreword to a forthcoming volume in the Uniform Edition.

Notes on Contributors

DANIEL AARON, b. Chicago 1912. Teacher, critic and literary historian. Professor of English at Harvard University. Author of *Writers on the Left* (1961), one of the most important studies of ideology and American literature during the inter-war years, and *The Unwritten War: American writers and the Civil War* (1973). He helped Elena Wilson on her edition of Edmund Wilson's *Letters on Literature and Politics* (1977) and wrote an introduction to it.

QUINTON ANDERSON, b. North Dakota 1912, son of playwright Maxwell Anderson. Teacher and critic. Professor of English at Columbia University and former head of Columbia's Department of English. His books include *The American Henry James* (1957) and *The Imperial Self* (1971), 'An essay in American literary and cultural history' about the role of the American preoccupation with self, with particular reference to Emerson, Whitman, Hawthorne and James. A seminal essay from *Kenyon Review* was reworked for *Scrutiny* (xv 1, 1947) at F. R. Leavis's request as 'Henry James, his symbolism and his critics', and inspired Leavis's essay 'Henry James and the function of criticism' in *The Common Pursuit*.

JACQUES BARZUN, b. France 1907. Critic and historian. Came to America in 1920 and studied at Columbia where he was Professor of History until his retirement in 1975. Currently he is literary adviser to Scribner's publishing house. His numerous books on literature and cultural history include *Teacher in America* (1945), the autobiographical *God's Country and Mine* (1954), and *Darwin, Marx, Wagner* (1958). An affectionate memoir 'Remembering Lionel Trilling' appeared in *Encounter* (September 1976).

M. C. (Muriel Clara) BRADBROOK, b. London 1909. Critic, theatrical historian and teacher. Educated at Girton College, Cambridge, and at various times Lecturer, Reader and Professor of English there, and Mistress of Girton 1968–76. She has written studies of *Joseph Conrad* (1941) and *Ibsen the Norwegian* (1947), and numerous books on the theatre, the most recent being *The Rise of the Common Player* (1962), *English Dramatic Form* (1965) and *Shakespeare – the poet in his world* (1978). She contributed to *Scrutiny* in its first two years. (for example, on William Empson) and several books of hers were later to be harshly dealt with there.

MORRIS DICKSTEIN, b. New York 1940. Critic and teacher. Professor of English at Queen's College of the City University of New York and contributing editor of *Partisan Review*. Educated at Columbia, Yale, and Clare College, Cambridge. His books include *Keats and his Poetry* (1971) and *Gates of Eden* (1977), an important revaluation of 'American culture in the sixties', where he writes about Trilling's relation to the political currents of the time.

STEPHEN DONADIO, b. New York 1942. Critic and teacher. Educated at Brandeis, he has taught English and comparative literature at Columbia, and is currently Associate Professor at Middlebury College, Vermont. Assistant editor of *Partisan Review* and author of *Nietzsche, Henry James and the Artistic Will* (1978).

JASON EPSTEIN, b. New York 1928. Publisher (vice-president of Random House) and radical journalist. Educated at Columbia University. As a pioneer of superior soft-cover publishing on America he brought out inexpensive editions of Edmund Wilson's essays as Vintage paper-backs. In 1963 he helped found the the *New York Review of Books* (which his wife Barbara Epstein co-edits) and is the author of *The Great Conspiracy Trial* (1970), a report on the trial of the Chicago Seven. His memoir 'Remembering Edmund Wilson' was published in the *New York Review of Books* (20 July 1972).

ROY FULLER, b. Failsworth, Lancashire 1912. Poet, novelist, critic and solicitor, he worked in the latter capacity for the Woolwich Equitable Building Society from the 1930s until the late 1960s. He has been a governor of the

BBC, a member of the Arts Council of Great Britain, and was Professor of Poetry at Oxford 1968–73. His several collections of verse include his *Collected Poems* (1962) and *The Reign of Sparrows* (1980). The second volume of his Oxford lectures on poetry, *Professors and Gods* (1973), deals extensively with F. R. Leavis.

MARTIN GREEN, b. London 1927. Critic, teacher and cultural historian. Educated at Cambridge and the University of Michigan, he is now Professor of English at Tufts University, Mass. Author of the partially autobiographical *A Mirror for Anglo-Saxons* (1959), and various works of speculative cultural history, among them *The Von Richthofen Sisters* (1974) and *Children of the Sun* (1976), both of which touch upon the work of F. R. Leavis within large national and international contexts.

JOHN GROSS, b. London 1935. Critic and literary journalist. Editor of the *Times Literary Supplement* since 1974, and formerly literary editor of the *New Statesman* (1972–74). He taught English literature at London University and Cambridge (Fellow, King's College 1962–5). His *The Rise and Fall of the Man of Letters* (1969) deals with F. R. Leavis, and his influential symposium *Dickens and the Twentieth Century* (co-edited with Gabriel Pearson in 1962) anticipated Dr Leavis's special interest in the novelist.

STUART HALL, b. Jamaica 1932. Teacher, writer and broadcaster. Rhodes Scholar at Oxford and since 1973 Director of the Centre for Contemporary Cultural Studies at Birmingham University where for some years he was a Research Fellow and Deputy Director under Richard Hoggart. A founding editor in 1957 of *Universities and Left Review* (later *New Left Review*) he has published articles and criticism in numerous journals. With Paddy Whannel he wrote *The Popular Arts* (1964), an influential study of popular culture and the mass media that prepared the way for their systematic study in schools.

D. W. (Denys Watt) HARDING, b. Lowestoft, Suffolk 1906. Academic psychologist and literary critic. Since 1969 Emeritus Professor of Psychology at the University of London, where he had taught since 1945, having previously been at Liverpool University. From 1937–47 he was on the editorial board of *Scrutiny* along with his former supervisor F. R. Leavis, and from 1948–54 was editor of the *British Journal of Psychology*. With Gordon Bottomley he edited the first edition of *The Complete Poems of Isaac Rosenberg* (1937), and he has written *The Will to Dominate* (1941) and *Experience into Words* (1963), a collection of essays on poetry, several of them from *Scrutiny*.

JOHN HOLLANDER, b. New York 1929. Poet, critic and teacher. Educated at Columbia University, and since 1976 Professor of English at Yale. His most recent collection of verse *Spectral Emanations* (1978) draws on books of poetry going back to the early 1960s. He has published several works of criticism and edited anthologies, including *The Oxford Anthology of English Literature*, of which he and Frank Kermode were general editors and to which Lionel Trilling contributed.

IRVING HOWE, b. New York 1920. Critic, historian and teacher. Educated at City College of New York and since 1963 Professor of English at Hunter College, New York. A founding editor of the radical journal *Dissent* in 1957, his many books include histories of *The American Communist Party* and *The United Auto Workers*, studies of Sherwood Anderson, Thomas Hardy and William Faulkner, and, most recently, the monumental *World of Our Fathers* (1975), published in Britain as *The Immigrant Jews of New York: 1881 to the present*, which brought him a National Book Award. He reviewed *Sincerity and Authenticity* for *Commentary* (August 1973) and published an appreciation of Lionel Trilling in the *New Republic* (13 March, 1976). The former is reprinted in his *Celebrations and Attacks* (1979), as is a review of Wilson's *Letters on Literature and Politics*.

ALFRED KAZIN, b. Brooklyn 1915. Critic, editor and university teacher. In 1942 he succeeded Edmund Wilson as literary editor of *New Republic*, and subsequently worked for *Fortune* (1943–4). He has held numerous academic appointments, and since 1963 he has been a Professor at the State University of New York. His principal work of criticism is *On Native Grounds: an interpretation of modern American prose literature* (1942), and he has published several collections of literary essays and edited numerous anthologies. His autobiographical trilogy, *A Walker in the City* (1951), *Starting Out in the Thirties* (1965), and *New York Jew* (1978), is an invaluable account of growing up in Brooklyn's Jewish community and the New York intellectual life of the past forty years. *New York Jew* contains an affectionate memoir of his friendship with Edmund Wilson and a somewhat acerbic one of his more limited acquaintanceship with Lionel Trilling. The latter, it should be said, has been contested by a number of Trilling's friends in a letter to the *New York Times*.

STEVEN MARCUS, b. New York 1928. Critic and teacher. Educated at Columbia University where he is now Professor of English. With his former teacher Lionel Trilling, he abridged Ernest Jones's biography of Freud. His books include *Dickens from Pickwick to Dombey* (1964), *The Other Victorians* (1966), a study of sexuality and pornography in the nineteenth century that rediscovered *My Secret Life* and introduced the word 'pornotopia' into the language, and *Engels, Manchester and the Working Class* (1974). He is an associate editor of *Partisan Review*. His article on Trilling in *New York Times Book Review* (8 February 1976) is reprinted in *Art, Politics and Will* (1977).

NORMAN PODHORETZ, b. New York 1930. Educated at Columbia and Clare College, Cambridge, and since 1960 editor of *Commentary*. His collection of literary essays and reviews *Doings and Undoings* (1964) includes his well-known piece 'The article as art' and two articles on Edmund Wilson. His autobiography *Making It* (1968) not only deals vividly with the New York literary world but with his studies under Trilling at Columbia and Leavis in Cambridge. His essay 'Arnoldian function in American criticism' (a review of *The Liberal Imagination*) appeared in the June 1951 *Scrutiny* (xviii, 59–65). He recently published a lengthy account of his involvement in the cultural politics of the sixties and seventies, *Breaking Ranks* (1979), in which Lionel and Diana Trilling both figure.

V. S. PRITCHETT, b. Ipswich 1900. Critic, novelist, short story writer, travel writer. His many books include *Collected Short Stories* (1956); *The Spanish Temper* (1957); portraits of London (1962), New York (1965) and Dublin (1967); studies of *Meredith and English Comedy* (his Clark Lectures at Cambridge, 1970), *Balzac* (1973) and *Turgenev* (1977); the two volumes of autobiography, *A Cab at the Door* (1968) and *Midnight Oil* (1971); and most recently *The Mythmakers* (1979), essays on Russian and Latin American authors. In the *New Statesman* (7 July 1972), the paper with which he was closely associated for over forty years until he rejected its new appearance and editorial policy in 1979, he wrote about 'My friend Edmund Wilson'. The previous year he reviewed Wilson's *Upstate* in the *New York Review of Books* (7 October 1971), and on 23 December 1972 he reviewed the revised edition of *To the Finland Station* for *The New Yorker*.

CHRISTOPHER RICKS, b. London 1933. Critic, teacher and editor. Professor of English and Fellow of Christ's College, Cambridge, since 1975. Formerly Professor of English at Bristol and Fellow of Worcester College, Oxford. Co-editor of *Essays in Criticism* , frequent contributor to the *Sunday Times* and BBC Radio 3. His books include *Milton's Grand Style* (1963), *Tennyson* (1972) and *Keats and Embarrassment* (1974). His Radio 3 obituary talk, 'Lionel Trilling and death', was published in the *Listener* (27 November 1975).

STEPHEN SPENDER, b. London 1909. Poet, critic and editor. Professor of English, University of London, since 1970; co-editor of *Horizon* 1938–41 and of *Encounter* 1953–65. Numerous collections of poems since 1934 including *Collected Poems* (1975), an autobiography *World Within World* (1951), and a series of essays with autobiographical notes covering forty years, and touching on his close friendship with W. H. Auden and Christopher Isherwood, *The Thirties and After* (1978).

GEORGE STEINER, b. Paris 1929. Educated at the University of Chicago and Balliol College, Oxford (Rhodes Scholar). Since 1974 Extraordinary Fellow of Churchill College, Cambridge, and Professor of English and Comparative Literature at the University of Geneva. His books include *Tolstoy or Dostoievsky* (1958), *The Death of Tragedy* (1960), *Language and Silence* (1967), in which he writes on F. R. Leavis, *In Bluebeard's Castle* (his 1971 T. S. Eliot Memorial Lectures), and *After Babel* (1975).

GORE VIDAL, b. West Point, NY 1925. Novelist, screenwriter, playwright and critic. His first novel, *Williwaw* (1946), drew on his wartime service in the Aleutians. His many subsequent novels include *The City and the Pillar* (1948), *Julian* (1964), and the political trilogy *Washington DC* (1967), *Burr* (1973) and *1876* (1976). His essay 'Ladder to Heaven: novelists and critics of the 1940s' originally appeared in *New World Writing 4* (1953) under the pseudonym 'Libra', and was collected in *Rocking the Boat* (1962). The review 'Edmund Wilson, tax dodger' was reprinted in his second collection of essays *Reflections on a Sinking Ship* (1969).

JOHN WAIN, b. Stoke-on-Trent 1925. Novelist, poet and critic, one-time lecturer at Reading University. Professor of Poetry at Oxford University 1973–8, and Fellow of Brasenose College. Numerous novels since the picaresque *Hurry On Down* (1953), several collections of verse including *A Word Carved on a Sill* (1956) and *Wildtrack* (1965), and various critical works including a substantial biography of *Samuel Johnson* (1974). He edited *An Edmund Wilson Celebration* (1978).

WILLIAM WALSH, b. London 1916. Critic and university teacher. Professor of Commonwealth Literature and Chairman of the Department of English at the University of Leeds. His books include *The Use of Imagination* (1959), and studies of *Coleridge* (1967), *R. K. Narayan* (1971) and *V. S. Naipaul* (1972).

YIGAEL YADIN, b. Jerusalem 1917. Soldier, statesman and archaeologist. At various times Chief of General Staff of Haganah, Chief of Staff of the Israeli Army, and Lecturer and Professor at Hebrew University, Jerusalem. In 1977 he became Deputy Prime Minister of Israel. Author of numerous books on aspects of the Dead Sea Scrolls including *The Scrolls and the War of the Sons of Light Against the Sons of Darkness* (1955), *The Message of the Scrolls* (1957), *Masada* (1966), and *The Temple Scrolls* (1977).

PHILIP FRENCH, b. Liverpool 1933. Writer, broadcaster and radio producer. Since 1959 he has been a talks and features producer for the BBC, working principally for what are now Radio 3 and Radio 4. His books include *The Movie Moguls* (1969) and *Westerns* (1974), and his articles and essays have appeared in numerous periodicals including the *New Statesman* (of which he was dramatic critic and arts columnist in the late 1960s), the *Observer* (of which he is movie critic), *The Times*, *Sight and Sound*, *Encounter*, *London Magazine* and the *Times Literary Supplement*. In 1972 he was a Visiting Professor at the University of Texas.